PENGUIN ANAN

THE F

A devotee of Sai Baba of Sh   ne of the
most influential spiritual writ   the author of
nineteen books, including the be   gy, which has been
translated into several languages.

In 2014, *Rabda: My Sigh . . .   y Sai*, published by Penguin
Random House India, was an instant bestseller.

A former journalist, Ruzbeh is also a documentary film-maker.
His documentary *Sehat . . . Wings of Freedom*, on AIDS and HIV in
Tihar Jail, was screened at the XVII International AIDS Conference in
2008. His collaboration with Zambhala—India's yoga, music and life
spirit festival, the first of its kind—gave birth to a series of powerful
videos called 'Ramblings with Ruzbeh Bharucha'.

His articles have been published in the *Times of India*, *Free Press
Journal*, *Indian Express*, *Maharashtra Herald*, *Sunday Observer*,
Jam-e-Jamshed and *Afternoon*.

His book *My God Is a Juvenile Delinquent* has been included in
the reading list of all judicial academies in India. Ruzbeh is the 110th
Master for the 'Speaking Tree', where he writes immensely popular
blogs on spirituality.

ICE with Very Unusual Spirits, a bestseller published by Penguin
Random House India in 2017, is still on Amazon's 'Best Reads' list.

His Facebook page has reached out to thousands in a very short
span of time. The daily affirmations and messages are a source of
inspiration to many.

You can reach him here:
Email ID: sairuzsai@rediffmail.com
Website: www.ruzbehbharucha.net
Facebook: www.facebook.com/ruzbehbharucha
Twitter: @ruzbehnbharucha
YouTube: www.youtube.com/channel/UCo-rFxiF7R9qaMMWdpj5fJQ
Speaking Tree: https://www.speakingtree.in/ruzbeh-bharucha/

ALSO BY THE AUTHOR IN PENGUIN ANANDA

The Fakir

The Journey Within

RUZBEH N. BHARUCHA

PENGUIN
ANANDA
An imprint of Penguin Random House

PENGUIN ANANDA

USA | Canada | UK | Ireland | Australia
New Zealand | India | South Africa | China

Penguin Ananda is part of the Penguin Random House group of companies
whose addresses can be found at global.penguinrandomhouse.com

Published by Penguin Random House India Pvt. Ltd
4th Floor, Capital Tower 1, MG Road,
Gurugram 122 002, Haryana, India

First published in Penguin Ananda by Penguin Random House India 2020

Copyright © Ruzbeh N. Bharucha 2020

All rights reserved

10 9 8 7 6 5 4 3 2

This is a work of fiction. Names, characters, places and incidents are either the
product of the author's imagination or are used fictitiously and any resemblance
to any actual person, living or dead, events or locales is entirely coincidental.

ISBN 9780143450214

Typeset in Bembo Std by Manipal Technologies Limited, Manipal

Printed at Manipal Technologies Limited, India

www.penguin.co.in

BABA WINCED AS He sipped the tea made by Rudra.

'I, The Fakir, the very God to countless of my children, who can perform miracles that make the very heavens sigh with wonder, have failed miserably in teaching you how to make a respectable cup of tea. What a tragedy!' He took another sip and sighed. There was a twinkle of a smile in His Divine eyes.

'You too seem to have failed rather spectacularly where your attempts at humour are concerned, oh Lord and Master of the Universe,' Rudra said as he prepared the chillum for Baba. He took a few drags to strengthen the fire element and then passed the chillum to Him.

Baba took a deep puff, inhaled and sighed again.

'But there are not many in this entire universe who can prepare a chillum like you, Rudra-ji.'

'I am so humbled that if my very toes could weep they would weep now, Baba.'

Blondie, the dog, walked in, tail wagging, looked at both the men, sat down beside Baba and with her paw sought Baba's attention. Baba caressed the girl. As if on cue the other two dogs, named *Boy* and *Girl*, walked in and after a while found their respective places in the room. The sun had set forty-five minutes ago and Baba had finished His customary prayers while Rudra tinkered away in the kitchen. This was their daily routine. Sunset meant prayers for Baba. Rudra prepared his controversial chai, with lemon grass, while the coal for the chillum was readied. They then sat and drank tea and passed the chillum around. Once it got dark they would walk on the beach and say their respective prayers.

The rules applied as always. Rudra was not to speak to Baba when with other people. He was to behave as if Baba was not even present. Thus any sort of an introduction was out of the question which was rule number two, followed by rule number three: Rudra should not mention his interaction with Baba to anybody.

The rule of eating one meal a day at some café, where there was human company, was relaxed. Now it was thrice a week. Rudra continued to eat at Martins', the establishment run, managed, served by the formidable Martins' with their crew who had last smiled when India had become an independent nation. Even now after two years or more of Baba and Rudra's first meeting, the only sign of familiarity was that they had assigned Akbar, a chap who was as gregarious and forthcoming as a defunct signboard, to serve Rudra. He mumbled the day's menu and Rudra would mumble back what he wanted to eat and then would read the papers while he ate his food, tipped the sourpuss, then one of the Martins' would grunt a goodbye and that was that. Sometimes those who knew Rudra or of Rudra would come and speak for a while or take time for channelling.

Oh yes, the fourth and last rule still applied. Rudra would do all the housework on his own except when it had anything to do with electricity, carpentry or plumbing. Baba would so often remind Rudra that he would rather drink his lousy tea than see his feeble, confused attempt at housekeeping.

Thus every night Baba and Rudra would go for a stroll and, upon their return, as Baba rarely ate dinner, maybe a buttered toast dunked into tea, both the men would pray and talk through the night. Baba would often take Rudra on an astral voyage and Rudra would do as he was told during those journeys. Earlier it was fascinating, but now, it was like entering another room and taking care of innumerable people with virtually similar problems.

There were different kinds of issues that mainly related to problems of money, anger, greed, lust, betrayal, fear, playing the victim, being unreasonable, fights, loneliness, sadness, spiritual queries and the innumerable usual things afflicting all living beings. Mostly the issues were about Karma dished out to all beings with not much thought or emotion. As Baba would so often say, 'Karma is not our enemy . . . Karma is our greatest friend . . . Karma when embraced joyously leads to salvation and liberation . . . but being ignorant we fight our best well-wisher with the cloak of anger, hate and negativity; we push away the one who only wants the eternal best for each of us instead of embracing all that our friend wants us to experience— Wake up, Rudra! Don't you dare snore when I speak such powerful words to you, you rascal.'

Rudra's life had not changed. He channelled for those who came for help and over a number of people came over. It tired Rudra but that is understandable as everybody came with problems and Rudra tried his best to divine the solutions or figure out ways of dealing with the ordeal. Sometimes the Karmic blueprint could suddenly get altered which upset people as that meant the predictions were not transpiring into reality but most often people came back which only meant that things were on track. Since a while Rudra only focused on emergencies and spiritual queries but miracles were taking place, thanks to Baba.

Rudra channelled as and when there were people who wanted help but he had kept a few days for divination. He did not want people to begin using him as a crutch and he had no intention of having a following or, God forbid, a cult. Thus, he purposely restricted his séances to a few sessions in the week. That way those who truly needed help were provided with solace and comfort, and divination; especially those who were walking the Path.

He still did not charge people any money but most people often left gifts and money which took care of Rudra's needs and even wants. Mr Seth converted Rudra's black van into a beautiful house on wheels, very comfortable, but from outside it looked the same as Rudra did not like attracting attention.

Rudra did not interact with the outside world apart from his cottage landlord, Dwarka. His landlord was an elderly man living his last days in New Zealand, more than happy that Rudra had leased his cottage and was taking good care of it. He had nobody to leave the cottage to and had indicated to Rudra that if all went as planned he would *will* the cottage to Rudra as long as Rudra kept aside the rent to help elderly people who were in need.

Baba Sai and he went for a stroll. When alone in the dark, with the cool sea breeze and the soothing sound of the waves with nobody around, Baba spoke to Rudra about life, taught him prayers and talked about this and that and everything, many a time about things that Rudra could not share with another being.

Life was simple. Life was cool.

Karma is not our enemy . . . Karma is our greatest friend . . . Karma when embraced joyously leads to salvation and liberation.

VERY OFTEN BABA would disappear for a few days and Rudra realized that on those days he was unusually preoccupied with some mundane things. Stuff that needed to be sorted out in the cottage or he was simply not in the zone to do anything and be dazed, all appointments cancelled, he preferred being by himself. He never understood how every time Baba would leave, Rudra's days were either packed with worldly chores or just depressing.

On those days he drank far more than he should but always outside the cottage, never within its holy premises. He always made sure the oil lamps burnt twenty-four seven, and Baba would light a small fire, mainly burning embers, which Rudra would tend to in order to always keep the fire awake. Without Baba's physical presence Rudra was lost, though he knew that he should not be as Baba was always with and within him.

Rudra always remembered Baba's words to him. He had told him in the early days of their meeting, 'Beta, heaven is filled with those who have failed but who have got back on their feet, dusted off their mistakes and follies, smiled and walked on with The Name on their lips and the comfort of a compassionate heaven in their hearts.'

Rudra missed serving Baba and massaging His feet. When Baba was physically with him Rudra's day would be remarkably the same, making sure Baba was taken care of, from the innumerable cups of chai to hot bowls of soup to prayers and laughter and conversations ending the day with him massaging Baba's feet. He loved to massage His feet.

The last time when Baba had left, there was a tremendous forest fire in California. Rudra always noticed that whenever Baba would leave the cottage, some place in the world would be going through unusual turmoil or devastation. It was as though He was needed and He had to be alone. Rudra never pried or questioned Baba. Rudra just served silently and joyously.

Blondie, Boy and Girl never left Rudra's side when Baba was not present. It was as though they understood that he was alone and they rallied around him and sought his attention. On those days, Rudra would give them a bath and pedicures and pamper them as he needed to be active to prevent the ache felt in his heart because of Baba's absence.

Heaven is filled with those who have failed but who have got back on their feet, dusted off their mistakes and follies, smiled and walked on with The Name on their lips and the comfort of a compassionate heaven in their hearts.

BABA RETURNED AND life got back to its normal routine. After dinner Baba motioned to Rudra that they should take a stroll on the beach. There was nobody. It was late at night. The sky was pregnant with countless stars and it was two days till full moon, thus, the beach was lit with a soft radiant moonlight and the sea was withdrawn within herself and one could hear the music of the waves but at a distance.

'I know you want to ask me questions about life and all the usual queries most of mankind wants to know about. This is as good a time as any, ask and you shall be left astounded, my sweet demented child.'

Rudra smiled and said nothing. He loved his Master. As usual his Master knew everything.

'Okay, my Lord of the universe, tell me something about inherent tendencies? Where do they arise from and why are they so difficult to shed from one's deepest conscious and subconscious self?'

Baba walked in silence for a while. Then they sat down on the soft sand, facing the ocean, where moonbeams danced and made the water sparkle.

'Whatever we have nurtured in various lifetimes becomes cemented as inherent tendencies in the present lifetime. If, for instance, somebody has encouraged anger in some lifetime, then anger will be the dominant characteristic of an individual in this lifetime. If you have nurtured greed through lifetimes, the tendency to be greedy shall become the dominant force of an individual in this lifetime. Hate culminates into greater hate. Calmness worked upon shall lead to a soft tranquil disposition. Selflessness will lead to Oneness and compassion and platonic love. Slowly through lifetimes whatever emotion one works with will eventually cement that characteristic or emotion into an inherent tendency. Most often our negative inherent tendency rules our disposition and our traits. They become our character flaws. It is always easier to come down than go up. Gravity works in the same way. Anger will have more presence in an individual than peace, till anger is not prevalent and only peace reigns. Thus, we see people with greater character flaws than character strengths.'

'Then how do we go beyond our character flaws, Baba?'

'By first knowing who we truly are as individuals. When we know what our inherent strengths, weaknesses and limitations are and when we are honest about wanting to know our true self, only then can we begin to understand who we truly are as individuals. To know our inherent tendencies, good and not so good, we need to know who we genuinely are without any hypocrisy or deceit, walking the by-lanes of denial. Till this does not happen we shall never be really honest about our desire to better ourselves, and till we are not truly honest about knowing our true selves we shall never really see the Light but always dwell in the shadows of dark alleys. Living without knowing one's true weaknesses, strengths and limitations is like driving a very high-powered vehicle with eyes shut, feet pressing the speed pedal and hands off the steering wheel. Only disaster awaits the vehicle, the one behind the steering wheel and those in the vehicle. Thus, first and foremost know who you truly are. Without this no growth is truly possible. However deplorable the answers that might come forth in your search for your true self may be, it is important first to know who you are, as the journey can truly only begin once we are aware of who we are, what we are dealing with, what our strengths are, what are our weaknesses, our limitations and then with all the cards in our hands, then we focus on our strength, stay away from our weakness, and try to work on our limitations.'

'Do you really think we are capable of staring at the truth in the eye, especially of our own selves?'

'My sweet monkey, of course it is difficult and shall not come easy but it all depends on how serious you are and whether this is a true need, in fact a desperate need, an inevitable stepping stone in one's own growth and journey. It is hard, slow, heartbreaking going within the jungles of one's own dark self. You will also know at what speed to travel and work on yourself. You will be the best judge to decide whether you can slowly and slowly starve off your weaknesses and tendencies or you can severe them in one go or is it going to take years or maybe even a lifetime or more. But all this shall only happen when you know who you are and what you are truly dealing with.'

'Baba, how does one stay away from one's inherent pull of nature, maybe depression or anger or greed or hate or whatever. Even if I know it is my weakness, how does one work on it?'

'You sweet frog, when you know something is dragging you down, the first step is to stay as far away as possible from that emotion. Which means do not indulge in things that give greater power to that character trait! When you know something angers you, either prepare yourself not to react or admit you shall be angered, but still stay forcibly calm. Once you are equipped with self-realization of your nature and temperament, you are already forewarned of what is going to trigger anger, hate, depression, and if you are aware then you already are one up on that emotion.'

'Baba, it's easier said than done.'

'Of course, you silly mango, it is difficult but if your priority is to work on yourself then it is as easily done as said. To work on your inherent tendencies, one needs to make it one's soul and sole priority. One can go beyond one's negative tendency by not surrendering to its pull and destructive power. It eventually comes down to what is your priority. What is it that you want to surrender to? It comes down to the individual and how motivated and focused the person is to overcome or go beyond the inherent tendency. It is not going to be easy but you have to amputate the thing killing your very being. Whoever told you amputation was a breezy pastime? It's a life-altering decision. Each moment requires tremendous determination. Slowly but surely the grip of that tendency will loosen if you are persistent enough and you will be able to overcome the tendency or have enough power over it and through the years, the tendency might even starve and drop away. Remember, my sweet worm, each of us has to decide whom we want to prostrate ourselves in front of: The One we pray to and worship and believe in or our very mind. Our tendencies are all logged into our own vibration and consciousness which we call the mind. Remember the purpose of all negative tendencies is to pull us down but the true inherent nature of one's Spirit is to rise up. The more you allow the external tendencies to gain power, the deeper you shall sink and if the focus is on the Divine Spirit, the more you shall gravitate towards The One. Thus, the question to ask is 'Who am I?' Once you start this journey slowly the answers shall set you free. So in reality, you set yourself free. The joy of seeing the complete daftness on your face is worth the wonders of owning a few galaxies, my child. Come now let us just observe the stars and the moon and the shimmering water and set ourselves free from all thoughts and tendencies and life and all that.'

Rudra sighed. He began to massage Baba's feet and the Old Man exhaled in peace.

To know our inherent tendencies, good and not so good, we need to know who we genuinely are without any hypocrisy or deceit, walking the by-lanes of denial.

THAT NIGHT BABA took Rudra on an astral voyage to a mountain. It was a huge mountain where one could not see the top, but an ongoing mountain which clouds later covered. It was never-ending, had various plateaus and various inclines going as far as the eye could see, the mountain was sky-high. They climbed for a while and then Rudra was taken to a village. The scenery and the beauty of the place took his breath away. Rudra had never seen anything as picturesque as this place. It felt as though Rudra was in heaven seeing the beauty of paradise. But there was something wrong in the vibration of this place. As beautiful as it was, the vibration felt heavy and foreboding. Rudra saw people moving about their day-to-day affairs and then he understood why the very air seemed so dense and heavy. Everybody here was scared. There was an underlying stench of fear in this place. The contrast between the divinity and beauty of the place and the heaviness and denseness of vibration was so prominent that it made Rudra feel ill.

The most spectacular place where even the light was vibrant and inviting but in each individual, be it a child, woman, man or an animal, there was fear that lurked in their eyes and in their vibrations and aura. Rudra felt as though he was in heaven but covered with sludge from hell. **Each individual Rudra saw went about life as though worried that something will go wrong. So though there was laughter, it was half-hearted, as though everybody was scared that too much laughter could bring forth some calamity**. At every pace there was a need for peace but a menacing sense of fear made even the little peace something to be apprehensive about. People ate but Rudra could figure out there was no taste on their tongues. Everyone spoke softly. Most were as though hiding from somebody or the other. For all its luminous clarity and play of light, the breathtaking vistas and scenic view, this place made Rudra ill.

Baba entered various homes and then came out after a while. The windows of most cottages were curtained but still partially open. Allowing the luminous light to enter but never completely, worried if somebody would see those living within. Rudra could see people within but they never really came out in the open. Rudra began to gasp for air but all he could breathe in was fear and he realized that eventually nothing truly mattered but peace within each of us, which leads to a joyous life filled with laughter and lightness of heart.

Rudra wanted to go back home. He had gone to places which were truly gruesome and scary, but he understood the demands of the situation and was always comfortable doing whatever Baba wanted of him. Never had he come to a place which looked like heaven and had the unmistakable stench of hell. Like a child who looked like an angel but was Satan within, Rudra found this heavenly looking place disturbing and he wanted to be back in his cottage with his Baba.

In a matter of a thought, Rudra was back in his cottage with Baba sitting in front of him, eyes shut, and Rudra sat looking at his Master till the latter opened His eyes.

'Now you understand how important it is for us to realize the truth within. I could have explained this scenario to you or I could have made you live this scenario. Wanting to change and working towards change are two different worlds, beta. The most beautiful place in creation with the most fearful people in the world and what happens to that place. It repulses you. Why? Because the external and internal are in conflict. When you want change you shall experience life like this. On the outside it all will be beautiful or seemingly normal but within you there will be conflict, as now you are going beyond the normal, you are going beyond the appearance, you are going within, and within there shall be stench, dirt and sewage of the worst possible kind, but all within, nothing external and for a long period of time you shall have to live in this contrast or in the so called normalcy of the situation knowing very well what you are truly made of. Don't hate yourself or judge yourself. Work on yourself. To go beyond inherent tendencies or character flaws one needs compassion and patience, not anger and various complexes. Understand that everybody has flaws and strengths just as you; then slowly work towards strengthening yourself and slowly detaching yourself from your lower self. Slowly but surely you will reach where you have to be. Now punish me with your tea.'

Rudra continued to massage Baba's feet for a while and then stood up and entered the kitchen. He put the water to heat and put a piece of coal for the chillum. He was glad to be home with Baba. Nothing else mattered to him but having his Master with him. Life was good. Life was cool.

Wanting to change and working towards change are two different worlds.

THE DAY PASSED fast. A few people had come for help and after channelling Rudra sat to massage Baba's feet. Baba was in prayer and Rudra prayed along with Baba while he massaged His feet. After a few hours Rudra did housework and returned to Baba who continued to be in a state of prayer. Often Rudra was aware that Baba's body was present, He wasn't there in it. During those times Rudra sat in front of Him and prayed or simply sat and observed His Master.

In the night after their soup and chillum they went out for a stroll. Today the sky was filled with clouds and the moon played hide-and-seek, throwing brilliant white light on the beach and water, and then long intervals of darkness when clouds covered her radiance.

They sat on the beach away from the water and Baba motioned Rudra to ask whatever he wanted to inquire.

'Baba, why is it so important to do self-inquiry about one's own self and one's character?'

Baba looked at the sea for a while and then said a prayer and looked at Rudra.

'All that which is noble and good comes from this simple art of self-inquiry. Not only does one know their strengths but even knowing one's weaknesses and limitations creates a greater impact to their health of character. For example, a person starts to self-inquire. The individual realizes that he or she has certain inherent flaws. The person starts to work on correcting those flaws. What follows for every individual is a simple act of understanding that just as he or she is flawed, so are most people. If you know that there are many flaws within you and you are working towards correcting those flaws, you will come to the realization that everybody around you too has flaws. Now if you are working towards rectifying your flaws, you will understand how difficult it is to overcome these shortcomings. When you understand how difficult it is to overcome these shortcomings, even though you are trying so hard to go beyond these character flaws, you will slowly start understanding that others too are in the grip or claws of their inherent tendencies and their shortcomings. You will automatically become more understanding of not only their character traits but also towards your own journey to better yourself.'

'So what starts off as improving oneself leads to understanding how everybody is on the same journey, some knowingly and many still oblivious?'

'Yes, my monkey. **The more you work on yourself the more you realize how hard the journey is and thus, you inevitably become more compassionate towards the flaws and self-centredness of others**, as you realize that either they too are trying their level best or they are so oblivious of their own inherent tendencies that you slowly shall begin to wake them up too, to begin their individual journey. Thus, first and foremost you have begun your journey. You now are slightly more aware of your strengths, weaknesses, limitations and now you are also aware how steep the incline is of the climb and that it is many a time, one step forward, two backwards, and this process is not only for yourself but for everybody, so you begin to get more understanding too of others and yourself. This is the most important aspect of self-inquiry. It is not concerned with just your growth but it also involves the journey of others and your attitude towards their journey.'

Baba kept silent for a while and looked at the sea beyond. Rudra waited for Baba to continue.

'The journey of *who am I,* is thus the first stepping stone of not only knowing who you are but also becoming a more understanding human being, a more compassionate human being and also moving towards one's Goddess, God, and Guru. The better the human being becomes, the closer you get to The One. It's the only reality of life. You become better, you become filled with more *Shakti,* the primordial force within and outside, the Goddess Energy, who is beyond the beginning and the end, who is the One who allows each of us to live our destiny and eventually merge back within Her. Some call Her, Ahura, some Devi, some God, some Allah, some Shakti, whatever you call Her; She is the creator, preserver and the destroyer, in reality the essence of everything.'

Rudra nodded. His love for Goddess Kali was known to Baba and Baba had revealed to Rudra often who the Primordial One truly was, is and has always been and will be.

'So what starts with a self-inquiry, makes you understand yourself better. With you understanding yourself better you begin to understand others far more than what you would have otherwise. With you identifying yourself and your journey with others you become a little more compassionate towards others. Compassion leads to a very important place in one's spiritual journey as it leads you to becoming less judgemental towards others. Remember, the real journey begins when one can't bear the darkness in their being and soul. That is when the search for Light commences. Once you are in search of Light, without doubt it will make you open your eyes to your own shortcomings and with that make you less judgemental about the shortcomings of others. So now you are more compassionate and less judgemental. Can you begin to understand the change in the individual's personal growth? All started with the inquiry of one's own self.'

'Baba, You mean all those who start on the journey of self-inquiry will all of a sudden become better human beings?'

'Yes, idiot child of mine. But remember this inquiry has to truly come from within. The need to know who you truly are should be like an insatiable hunger, eating your very core and it is then that this change becomes inevitable. It shouldn't be just some process for the reason of an exercise. You should want to change for the better by knowing yourself the best and then once the answers are with you then you need to work with the raw material to help you create a better you, working with your strengths, keeping a distance from your weaknesses and converting your limitations into something that will help you become a stronger and a better human being. This transformation to make yourself a better human being or to make your Goddess, God and Guru, more happy and proud of you, should be a desperate need and an insatiable want. Remember what you are doing: you are cleansing your energy within you, allowing the Goddess's Energy to recreate you. In fact, this is like a new birth that shall take place. From a caterpillar you shall be transformed into a butterfly. It shall be achieved with your need for change and the Goddess's blessings to fill you up with Her Energy, Her Shakti to make the change not only possible but also permanent. Her Energy makes things permanent. Remember, eventually for such a transformation to take place you need the blessings of The One but you need Her Energy, Her Shakti. This evolution is revolutionary. It is like, for the first time, coming face to face with Fire in the depth of the night in the densest of forests. It is not for the faint-hearted. Sometimes you will have to take steps that will go against all you have stood for or all that which you thought was normal or justifiable. This change might make you take certain decisions which you would not dare give any energy to in your wildest of dreams. This Shakti will make you into another human being in order to become a better human being. Sometimes one needs to be ruthless to be tender, one needs to be cruel to be kind. Such changes will happen naturally when you walk this Path of self-inquiry.

There will often be resistance from those around you because you are now transforming, and transformation is not an easy process for either the person in the throes of that transformation or for those who are close to the individual. You are becoming somebody else, somebody better, but that change might not be palatable to everybody or a few from the inner circle. But you have to evolve into a better human being and for that if you have to take decisions which could even be harsh, so be it, do it gracefully and with compassion. The Shakti burning within you will guide you but your role is to walk the Path. Let us take for example that you have become more compassionate to those who have not treated you well. You have become more understanding. You have even forgiven those who have done you harm. You might be called a hypocrite as earlier your stance was aggressive, even militant. Now it is soft and giving. Or it could completely be the other way round. Earlier you have allowed people to walk all over you but now you know that is unacceptable for the betterment of not only yourself but also those who have taken advantage of you. So you have become what they might term as being harsh, cold, ruthless, but you know it is for the highest good for all concerned. You have to keep walking the Path, beta, there is no other way. Darkness has power only in the absence of Light but all the darkness in the world cannot overpower a humble lit matchstick. You have to first become the humble lit matchstick until you become the Light itself. Wake up, Rudra, I know you aren't sleeping. Don't you snore, boy! Rascal!'

Rudra smiled. They both stood up and walked back to the cottage. Rudra slept near Baba's feet while The Old Man continued to pray.

Remember, the real journey begins when one can't bear the darkness in their own being and soul. That is when the search for Light commences.

THEY CLIMBED THE mountain a little further. They left that beautiful town with fear at every breath and now, after a while, they reached a village where everybody seemed to be hard at work. The village was not particularly picturesque. It was like any village one would drive through while in India. Nothing outstanding about this village but Rudra felt a sense of freedom. Everybody was hard at work. Children played noisily. The very elderly sat in the shade of large trees, smoking and talking amongst themselves. The young men and women worked in the fields. It was an everyday sight in countless villages but Rudra felt at home. Baba and he walked from home to home, most often nobody could see them. Baba did what He had to and Rudra did what he was directed to do. Most often there was cleansing of homes to be done and vibrations of people to be cleared. Nothing major, just run-of-the-mill aura cleansing. Rudra did notice that in many homes and farms where they did the aura cleansing, certain individuals were grappling with issues of guilt and anger, mainly self-directed.

Then Baba and Rudra sat under a tree and Rudra lit the chillum and passed it to Baba. After both smoked, Baba smiled and prayed for a while.

'Many a time, self-inquiry leads to guilt and anger directed towards the individual trying to learn one's own self. It is common to begin to dislike one's own self when one is learning to get to know oneself a little better. It doesn't make sense as here we are trying to remove weeds not planting seeds of discord. No matter what you have learnt of yourself, the first step is calm acceptance of one's lot. Till one does not come to calm realization and acceptance of oneself, the journey can never really begin. No matter how much you want to change for the better. No matter how deep the desire for self-inquiry. No matter how determined to better one's own self may be, if you do not learn to accept whatever one has learnt of oneself calmly, the journey shall not proceed ahead. You shall go about in circles. You might even begin to hate yourself and that shall in fact take you backwards. Thus, it is important to first calmly accept who one is and then with calm acceptance learn to better one self. This is most important, child. Do not flog yourself. You shall achieve only regret and remorse. **First learn to accept yourself and then with acceptance begin to correct yourself**. Don't get sucked into the dark abyss of guilt but after calmly accepting yourself begin to walk forward, slowly spreading the Light within to dispel darkness. This is what usually happens with the process of self-inquiry. Guilt and anger enter and very often the entire process leads to defeat due to anger and guilt. Do you understand, my child with the daft look?'

'Yes, Lord and Master of the chillum.'

'So my sweet gnome, for most the process of self-inquiry starts and ends with guilt and anger and the person quits the process, feeling the climb impossible. Convinced that with so much darkness, there is no way Light shall clear the Path. This is the first folly. A very dangerous mistake which should be avoided at all cost. However horrible an individual feels he or she is, the moment you accept yourself calmly, then and only then can change begin to take place. Drop-by-drop the ocean is filled. Never ever forget this. Energy has no emotion. Like water, it takes the shape of whatever intent we imbibe it with. So you can accept calmly whatever is in store for you or you can lash out and make a greater mess of the situation. The power to evolve or destruct is in the hands of each individual. The power of free will is many times greater than the power of destiny and the very Gods themselves.'

'So how do we go beyond the guilt and anger and complexes, Baba, as I am sure the deeper we dig within our own selves we are going to surface with lots of baggage and dirt?'

'My sweet fruit cake, always remember that the lower energies want to make you a vehicle to create disharmony and chaos, as that is their food and subsistence. Lower energies are present everywhere as the doors of paradise are shut to such energies and they roam about in the fringes of creation feeding off the uncentredness of all living beings.'

'Which means?'

'My daft child, it means that every time an individual wants to walk the Path, there are innumerable energies that do not want the person to succeed. Remember there is a war going on. Never forget this. The war between good and not good is always prevalent. **There will always be those who want others to follow their path of madness and selfishness and dark energies. They find safety in numbers. They will do everything possible to pull you down to their level**. They will not stop no matter how high you rise. They do not want the individual to soar but to be sucked into the abyss of darkness and negativity. Countless lower mindsets will try and bring you down but only when the individual is clear about his or her destination and priority will the individual succeed in evolving.'

'The process of self-inquiry will bring forth lots of angst and pain and undesirable truths to the understanding of the individual. Those who are clear that they will bear the cross and still walk forward, will move ahead, but those who get caught in the web of guilt and anger and self-reproach will never be able to surface out of the muck into the Light. It is as simple or as difficult as it sounds. If you allow yourself to be flogged, coming forward from some inane sense of vengeance against one's own self, you will sink deeper and faster into the sludge. The first step is always the most difficult as it involves a journey where the clarity of the Path or reaching the destination are still in a blur. But when your vision is clear, to rise above the muck and soar, heaven bound, only then will you break free from the clutches of the lower energies and self-incrimination. As I have told you so often, do not flog yourself because then you will achieve nothing but remorse and regret. Even remorse and regret to a particular degree are fine as long as you are going to use it to better yourself and move forward. But if you are going to use remorse and regret to just go on flogging yourself, out of some sense of self-punishment, it shall be of no use, as that self-punishment is not beneficial as it shall not let you rise but in fact sink you deeper into a sense of hopelessness. You can, for lifetimes, blame yourself for being a horrible human being or you can say, enough is enough I shall become a better human being. The choice is yours. But change is so difficult that many use this self-incrimination as an excuse and keep flogging themselves, continue to wallow in self-pity and also continue to resort to the life they have lived which even though now seemingly they hate. If you hate your previous life then change. Who stops you from change but yourself?'

'Understand who you are and then move forward towards the Light and eventually you too shall become the Light. It is a difficult process but then if you want to metamorphose into a butterfly, then be prepared for the initial discomfort and angst. Walk boldly knowing that you might fall but be aware that to rise again is in your hands and is in your favour. Fear cannot touch those who have faith in the Divine and faith in the fact that divinity can never be wrong. The wise know the difference between their needs and their wants. The need may be for self-centredness but want may be for selflessness. Then pursue selflessness even though it shall be a process of angst and trials. Once you know the difference and are clear where you want to reach, trust me son, you shall reach that place, slowly but surely.'

'But, Baba, it is a difficult path. Even when we go beyond self-accusation, guilt and anger, the journey is still not easy. There has to be change at every step and change, or any transformation for that matter, is never easy.'

'Yes, my boy. First we need to go beyond anger and guilt and self-blame. Then comes another difficult mountain to climb: keeping realistic aspirations and goals. One of the greatest pitfalls on the path of spirituality is setting unrealistic schedules and milestones. Know yourself and what you are capable of and then set your goals. Not based on speed or some fancy, but based on the reality of your own strengths, weaknesses and limitations. Oscillation in our spiritual pursuits is very often our greatest enemy. This comes about when we set unrealistic goals which come about when we still do not truly understand our true selves. So the first step after we have gone beyond self-reproach is to set realistic goals for ourselves. If an individual gets angry a hundred times a day, the first step would be to realistically reduce the times one gets angry in a day. Usually a wise person would start by resisting anger a few times less than normal, so as to bring the number of outbursts down to say ten times. **Thus, instead of getting angry a hundred times a day, you pledge to reduce your outbursts by ten to get the figure of ninety times a day of outbursts**. Then slowly bring it down by twenty, till you reach a stage where you, maybe, get angry twice a day. But it has to be done slowly and steadily. Now imagine the person declaring on the first day itself that instead of getting angry a hundred times a day, from today I shall get angry only twice a day. It will lead to chaos within the individual. Of course, there are people who can completely go into a silence zone and succeed but those individuals are rare. For a common person, start with realistic goals and slowly but surely come to a stage where outbursts are far spaced, till the individual reaches a point where maybe he or she could even go through days without a single outburst. Thus, it is important to set goals that are realistic and only when you know yourself well will you know what kind of goals are realistic and what aren't. The way forward is by clearing the backlog. **Sometimes one might even need to take a step backward in order to leap ahead**. So the individual might say that a hundred times a day itself is with a lot of restraint so for a while I shall not exceed the figure hundred. Then slowly start reducing the times of outbursts. It's a very individualistic approach. Often, the freshness of the fruit depends on knowing when to pluck it, how to store it and when to eat it. Similarly, choose your battles, knowing your strengths and weaknesses and limitations and then set the bar, not too high but just high enough. The bar should neither be too high, nor too low, nor should it be out of reach. Haven't I told you often, the wise know when to speak, how much to speak, how to speak, but most importantly, when to shut up. Often knowing when to keep quiet is more important than even speaking itself.

When a spoon of sugar can do the work, why waste a gallon of vinegar?'

'By being aware of who we are and mindful of our thoughts, words and actions, we save ourselves from the grief and chaos caused by the futility of unaware reactions. Remember, my sweet crazy child, eventually each drop is going to decide the quality of the goblet of milk that you offer to The One. However much you take care of the milk, if a drop of lime falls into that goblet, the milk will curdle. The cosmos is trying to teach us how careful we need to be on this Path. That one drop of lime can change the very essence of what you want to offer. Thus, on this journey, go slow, be steady, always sure, aware, and then take a step at a time. Do not be in a hurry. Haste will bring you back to where you started or worse, further back than from where you started. You don't want your life to be one step forward and two steps back, at every given step of your life.'

'Pure intent if not backed by sensible action is similar to a strategically placed well, filled with sludge and murky water. Rather useless to one and all. Also, when we realize that we all are work-in-progress, one becomes less judgemental to one's own self as well as to everybody else. That is the first step towards Oneness. Oneness starts with the realization that we all are in the same boat, some ahead, some in between, some behind, but all in the same boat, all moving towards the same destination.'

'But, Baba, the mind never really lets an individual move forward. It overwhelms all those trying to walk the straight line. Let us take for example the person who has done self-inquiry and even gone beyond guilt and self-reproach but the mind never stops pushing the individual at every step to go further down or go about in circles or go astray. What is to be done with the mind?'

Baba stood up and Rudra followed. They began to walk back towards the cottage. Baba was in prayer and Rudra realized that the talk for the day had ended. It could resume after a few minutes or days, it was all left to Baba. They entered the cottage and Rudra put the water to boil and coal to heat for another round of chai and chillum. Living with Baba, sleep sometimes was a rare visitor and when Baba wanted it to be, Rudra would sleep soundly for hours at a stretch. It all depended on what Baba wanted out of him. Rudra had long realized that his life was not his own and he wanted it no other way.

By being aware of who we are and mindful of our thoughts, words and actions, we save ourselves from the grief and chaos caused by the futility of unaware reactions.

THEY WERE BACK on the mountain. Another village, nothing special about this village, but there was a strange energy in the air. All were tilling the land. Some did so with a smile on their faces. Some with anger, while others with calmness. Some with worry while some with fear. Some with joy while some with a frown. They all were doing the same work but their expressions differed. Quite a few, you could see, had already lost interest and some thought the job impossible. You could see a few go about it peacefully, not in any rush, not trying to prove a point but many went about it with an aggression that you realized could not last. It was over eagerness but there was no way they could sustain such a tempo for too long. Most of them did the tilling but their minds were someplace else. Over here everything that was visible and revealed the person's state of mind. It was apparent. Nothing was hidden here. Nobody could lie or pretend; you got what you saw. Their state of internal being was projected outwards. Unlike on earth, in this place everything was stark nude. No place to hide and pretend.

Rudra spent time only with those who calmly went about their work. When they rested he sat with them and spoke about life and work and ate simple fare along with them. Nobody was more affluent or poorer than the other. It was a state of equality where only how you went about your life and day and thoughts made you different. Everything was dependent on the individual. Baba went about amongst those who seemed most rattled, those who seemed defeated, those who seemed to be engulfed by anger, guilt and a sense of hopelessness. Some responded by calming down and then going about their work calmly but many, in fact, got more desolate and tempered. Even Baba could not get through their state of agitation. He would smile but in that smile there was reverberation of heartbreak.

Rudra walked through the village and he noticed this stark openness of thoughts follow him. From children to the aged, they were all an open book. He could read every individual and it saddened him to see how most of them were engulfed by their state of mind, hopelessness, anger, guilt and recrimination. He wanted to tell them to drop these cloaks and wear the one of calmness but it was of no use as they had made up their minds and now even Baba could do nothing for most of them. They were all good people wanting to change but for many the change seemed so impossible a mountain to climb that they sank deeper into the void of gloom.

Of course, there were many who were glowing due to their process of self-evolvement. They went about their day calmly, slowly moving on their path, happy that they knew where they wanted to go and where they wanted to reach. For a few the task was Herculean but their state of mind allowed them respite from the state of hopelessness. Sometimes even the things that seem impossible become a ray of hope to strive towards. They took one step at a time hoping that drop-by-drop they would fill their own empty chasm and make an ocean out of virtual nothingness. Rudra realized that those who were calm had truly little going for them, their sense of calmness made the impossible seem possible. Rudra knew the importance of control of the mind and taking life one step at a time, one breath at a time. The state of calmness determined the state of sanity which determined how each moment was going to be either embraced or battled with.

This village taught him the need to know oneself and go about life with a state of serenity. This village was a mirror which reflected to Rudra the power of being at peace with each moment, which led to a bouquet of stillness which allowed the individual to grow and rise slowly upwards with a centredness that made life along with all its ups and downs worth breathing in.

In a flash, they were back in the cottage. All day Rudra met people and by evening, he was exhausted. But it was a good exhaustion, with sweetness to the tiredness that only comes about with honest, selfless work. They had soup at night, Baba prayed and spoke little and Rudra spent the night a bit in prayer but mostly serving Baba, making countless cups of tea, rounds of chillums, massaging His feet, making sure the oil and the wicks for the lamps were as they ought to be.

The next two days Baba was in silence and Rudra went for lunch to Martins' where he ate little but was content to be in the same space as that of other mankind. He drank only when Baba was physically out of the cottage. In reality he did not miss or crave for alcohol. Baba never told him not to drink. His focus was always on how to or how not to live or think or speak, never on how not to eat or drink something. Baba's focus was always internal, never external. His focus was always on how to live, not on how to get caught in the physicality of this or that. His teaching was simple: come from the centredness of each moment and do not let your reaction guide you for even a second. Be proactive, never reactive. Be silent rather than slander. Be kind, be generous, be selfless and if nothing, just be. It was difficult many times. Especially when you got to know somebody speaking ill of you, somebody who you trusted break your trust, and someone who you thought was your well-wisher was nothing but a flake in the wind. Baba would say then, it is most important now to be centred, if not now, then when? It is easy to be centred when all is going for you. That is not centredness, that is just basking in the sun. Centredness is when nothing is going for you and you are still within, silent, strong, controlled, part of the world, when every cell within you wants to be alone and to just be within.

'Baba, You are so funny.' Rudra would have tears in his eyes and Baba would chuckle and say, '*Sab theek hain, bachha, fikar mat kar.*'

Come from the centredness of each moment and do not let your reaction guide you for even a second. Be proactive, never reactive. Be silent rather than slander. Be kind, be generous, be selfless and if nothing, just be.

IT WAS NIGHT. Baba, Rudra, Blondie, Boy and Girl took a stroll on the beach. They had just finished with their dinner. Baba had His chai and chillum and now they walked slowly on the beach. The moon was waning but still bright and the sky was clear of any clouds. The sea sparkled and the waves played its music and all seemed well with the world. For a while they walked in silence and then Baba halted and sat down on the dry sand. Boy and Girl ran around while Blondie sat next to Baba and Rudra.

'The other night you had asked a question regarding the mind, as to the mind never stopping to push the individual to go astray from the moment and what is to be done about this, yes?'

'Yes, Baba.'

'Beta, no matter who you are, always remember that you cannot fight the mind. **You should not try to fight the mind**. Let us take for example that I heat a piece of coal and it's burning hot and I place the hot coal on your palm. What would you or anybody do? Logically the person would immediately make sure the coal is dropped and you are not in contact with it. Nobody would clutch the burning coal tight and hold on to it. **Thoughts are like burning coal and surprisingly**

most people hold on to the burning coal tightly and then complain that they have got burnt or disturbed or injured by that burning piece of coal. Thoughts that are like the pieces of burning coal can either be discarded immediately when one comes in contact with them or one can hold on and bear the consequences. In reality, it is not the thought or the burning coal that creates discomfort but it is how one handles the burning coal or thought that is going to decide the outcome. Either you chuck the coal away instantly or you hold on to it and suffer the consequences. It is, in reality, as simple or as difficult as this. Whether it's a piece of burning coal or one thought after the other, how you respond to that situation is going to decide whether you are going to be burnt or you are going to salvage yourself from the situation. Logically you should not want to hold on to the burning coal for even a second. When a thought comes about, we have three options. First is to not hold on to the thought; second is to fight the thought; third option is to encourage the thought. Either you chuck the piece of coal away, or you fight with the coal holding on to it, or you fan the burning piece of coal while you clutch at it. Every thought can be dropped and the mind can be diverted back to the moment or to something else or a chant or whatever it takes you to divert your mind from the thought; simply chuck it away. That is why it is so important to be in the moment because when you are in the moment, the burning coal is chucked away immediately when it makes contact with the skin or the self. The very moment the thought comes up, if one is aware, one chucks the thought away and one is free of the thought. It touches your skin and it is dropped away. You are free of that piece of burning coal the very moment it comes in contact with you. You are free. You are virtually untouched. You are unscathed. So this is the wisest way of handling thoughts. Each time a thought comes to you, you move on. Each time a thought assails you, you come back to your moment or to your breath or to your chant, or to whatever it takes for you not to hold on to the burning piece of coal.'

'Slowly the mind understands that you are not falling for the bait. Slowly the mind gets conditioned that you are one with the moment and its tricks will not work with you. Slowly the mind understands who the true Master is. Beta, it is a slow process and the mind never really stops placing pieces of burning coal but the frequency and intensity and duration all starts dwindling down. You can spend days without the mind playing its tricks. It shall keep trying but the frequency will reduce. You will spend days without a piece of burning coal being placed on your palm. Are you understanding what I am saying, my goat?'

'Yes, Lord and Master of the coal of mine.'

'Rascal! Now comes the situation where instead of dropping the coal the individual clutches it tightly and starts fighting with the piece of coal with the fist clutching the hot energy. The person is in agony but instead of letting go, the idiot is clutching on tighter to the burning ember. What is going to ensue? The person is going to get burnt. So when a thought comes about which one should drop immediately, but instead one fights the thought, one is not released off the thought but instead is burnt by the thought, the individual still refuses to let the thought drop away. Discomfort and agony shall ensue. The ember shall stick to your palm that now is formed into a closed fist. So when a thought comes that you do not want, instead of chucking it away, you are fighting it—this only means you are holding on to it tighter. We are not letting go, we are fighting it, by holding on to it. Who does that in real life? We would call that person silly who holds on to fire, screaming in discomfort but still refuses to let go of that piece of burning coal. In reality most people are doing the very same with their thoughts. Fighting them in discomfort rather than releasing the ember with ease. The more you fight the thought, in reality, the more you are gripping it tighter, which only burns you further and further. Let go of that piece of burning firewood and release yourself from the pain, angst and discomfort, but no, we shall hold on and fight it. Nobody can win this battle as you are holding on to the very thing that is causing you pain. You want to let go of what is causing you pain not clutch tightly at it. So when a thought assails your sanity you come back to the moment by dropping that thought, not fighting it. Drop it, drop it, drop it, till the mind gets the message. It will, depending on how seriously you want to be free of that thought. Do not fight it, my child, you are holding on to burning fire. Even a sage will be burnt with fire. There are no exceptions here. It seems that you understand what I am telling you which itself is close to a miracle so we shall now go to the last alternative, fanning the fire, encouraging and nurturing the fire that burns you.'

'So either you drop the piece of burning coal or you fight it by holding on to the fire or you nurture the fire all the while it is burning you more and more intensely. The third alternative is when a thought enters you, instead of dropping it, you work on that thought, you offer it things that make the thought stronger, make the coal burn brighter and more intensely. Many people, if not most, commit this mistake. They encourage the thought by giving it attention and creating scenarios in the mind and alternatives and various ways of getting back and what not. This shall only make the thought grow stronger, the coal burn only more intensely. You actually allow yourself to be burnt with greater force as you are tending to the fire while it burns your palm. You could have easily chucked the burning coal away in an instant but now you are nurturing it while it burns you. Where is the sense in this action? Would you nurture fire burning you or would you instantly protect yourself? You would instantly protect yourself. The more you are in the state of awareness, the faster you will let go of the burning ember. The more preoccupied, the slower your reflexes will be. This is the way to work with thoughts. As I said earlier, it is as simple or as complicated as you want it to be. Thus, when a thought comes to you, you have the power to either delete it, fight it or encourage it. If the thought is not about one's over all well-being, ideally, one should let go of it immediately by either coming back to the moment or create a situation where the mind is free of that thought by immersing yourself in something that lets you free off that thought. **Divert yourself, if you cannot be one with the moment. Chant**. Occupy yourself with something that frees you of that piece of burning coal. Do not make the mistake of fighting it or encouraging it. That is a blunder as you are giving more strength to that thought. When you live in awareness, you automatically drop the thought. When you are preoccupied, you shall make the mistake of fighting or encouraging it. When you look at things with a calm mind, you will realize the futility of most thoughts and slowly free yourself from their clutches. Reactions will only make matters worse. Being calm is not only the right thing to do spiritually, but also the most intelligent and practical way to embrace the moment and be free from the clutches of thoughts. Remember, My son, being calm, content and in serene acceptance of each moment is a blessing even the very heavens aspire for. So fragile is our state of mind that a single thought, word or glance can rattle one's sanity or well-being. The only way out is to be in the moment calmly and focus on the Spirit within rather than the workings of the mind. The mind is a treacherous master but the most soothing aide. Do not let the mind have a hold over you. Let it always be the other way around. That can only happen when you are in the moment, in the womb of silence and awareness. Always know that all of heaven and beyond reposes in the womb of calm silence.'

'But, Baba, why is it that when we try and sit in silence there are more thoughts that assail us? When I sit for meditation often more thoughts come about ravaging my state of calmness to the extent that one is virtually scared of sitting for meditation?'

'My sweet firefly, first and foremost, initially never try and sit for meditation hoping to immediately come to a state of calmness or nothingness. Even when you sit for meditation, initially be in the moment, which is focus on your breath. Don't try and reach the state of nothingness as you are not equipped for such a state of emptiness yet. Be in the moment, means be with your chant or your breath. Focus on your chant or your breath, till you become your chant and your breath and then you dissolve into nothingness. Thoughts will come as you go deeper into your chant or your breath. Another thought will arise and another and another and you keep coming back home, keep coming back to your chant or your breath, keep at it, keep at it, till you become your very chant and your breath.'

'When we sit silently or go within, initially more chaos will reign. The mind does not want to be controlled. The mind wants to be the Master not the server. Thus, more thoughts will prevail. Like steam rising from the scorched earth when the rain pours down. But as the rain continues to fall, the fragrance of Mother Earth envelops us all. Silence is that fragrance. Just keep at it and the *khushboo* of silence will intoxicate. Just keep at it. The space between inhalation and exhalation is most important. In that space resides silence and in that silence resides The One. The greater the distance between inhalation and exhalation, the greater the silence reigns, the deeper you shall go within, and one day you will become silence yourself. The space between inhalation and exhalation is silence and that silence is Oneness. Thus, focus on your breathing and you automatically focus on The One.'

'Don't expect that you will immediately zone out of everything. How is that possible? Stillness needs to be worked on. Yes, the more you are in the moment through the day, the easier it will be for you to meditate and be in that moment. The less you are in the moment through the day, it shall be painful for you to meditate as the mind has been ruling you through the day. What makes you think that just because now you want to meditate and become one with the moment the mind is going to allow you such comfort so easily? One has to work for everything in life. Nothing ever is free, beta. Remember this always. There are no free meals in the cosmos. We all have to work for each meal of ours. You want the most exquisite meal, the meal of nothingness and Oneness, for free? How is that ever going to happen? You want the most expensive dish in the world free of cost and effort, no bachha, that is not going to happen. Under no cost are you or anybody so privileged that you can expect meditation, Oneness and nothingness to come without proper effort and dedication.'

Baba then stood up and with a soft smile began His walk back to the cottage followed by His brood. Rudra put water to boil, and now when he picked up the piece

of coal to be heated he held the coal with greater respect
than he ever had before.

One has to work for everything in life. Nothing ever is free.
Remember this always. There are no free meals in the cosmos.
We all have to work for each meal of ours.

THEY WERE ON the mountain, in another village and here everybody was busy in their work. There was a lot of noise and hustle and bustle but Rudra noticed that there was stillness in this sound. No matter what each individual did, the person was deep within the moment and completely absorbed in whatever it is they were occupied with. Children played with abandon but with complete Oneness with their game. The adults worked in the farm, fixated on whatever they did. Rudra could make out those who were with The One in the moment, with One in the moment, those who were chanting, and those who were trying their level best to be one with their chore. The vibration enveloping them was an obvious indicator of their involvement with the moment. The greater the Oneness the more released the person was of all thought, burden, anxiety and tribulation. Yes, there were a few who seemed absorbed but were far away from the moment and their aura showed their non-centredness. It did not matter what the individual was occupied in or not, the aura never lied. Those who fought to be in the moment were far away from the moment and those who were just calmly absorbed in whatever they did, their aura shone a beautiful radiance. There was a certain difference in this village. Not that the individuals were purer or more righteous, but there was definite calmness in this village that Rudra had never experienced before. The stillness enveloped him and made him calm and still too. The noise no longer disturbed him and in fact dissolved into the background of the fragrance of stillness. Rudra did not want to leave this simple village. He wanted to be here with Baba forever.

Baba and he walked through the lanes of this little village. They sat in the shade of a banyan tree, Baba lit a chillum and passed it to Rudra.

'When you really look at things with a calm mind, automatically you begin to realize the futility of many actions and desires. This makes you more within, more in the moment which makes you further calmer, which allows you to drop more and more things, till the true priority of your existence only remains. You discern your strengths, weaknesses and limitations further and go further within. It is like the cycle of nature. Calmness leads to further stillness. Restlessness leads to further chaos. Slowly our priorities begin to harmonize with each other. Earlier we discerned what our priorities were but often our spiritual, emotional, intellectual, financial, social and physical priorities may not be in harmony with each other. As you get calmer, harmony automatically sets in. You will realize that what you thought was a priority is nothing more than ego or a distraction. Slowly all the priorities begin to complement each other and work in harmony and that leads us closer to our destination and our eventual salvation. This is very important, beta. **Our priorities have to be in**

sync with each other otherwise it leads to greater discord. This we shall ascertain when we come from complete calmness and honesty within. So, once again we come back to our breath. The breath determines one's thoughts. Thoughts influence our words and thus our breath, thought, word become fuel for our deeds. Thus, it originates from the breath and leads to deeds that eventually give birth to Karma, which then opens up another cycle of cause and effect. It all starts with our stillness or restlessness and leads eventually to stillness or chaos. To go within isn't possible without calmness and calmness isn't possible without true acceptance that *You know best, so be it.* Everything is entwined and it starts with the inquiry of *who am I and what do I want to be and where do I want to reach?* When you come from calmness, peace and well-being to oneself and all, then everything else will follow. That shall lead to compassion and forgiveness. As you walk this path you shall use your free will to liberate yourself and also those who are knotted up with you in this eternal Karmic dance of give and take, cause and effect. It shall happen naturally. But it all has to start with knowing who you are and where do you want to reach. If peace is your priority then you will take the harshest of steps to achieve everlasting peace. You will not surrender for transient peace but only everlasting peace. Even if the world doesn't understand you and those you thought were yours go against you, you shall walk the Path silently. You shall walk the Path however hard and harsh it may be initially and you shall do it not only for yourself but for all concerned. This decision shall never be self-centred but all encompassing. But take the decision with a calm mind. When calm, nothing matters, and when restless, even heaven shall leave you disgruntled. I guess that is why there are earthbound souls as even heaven cannot change their minds and their insistence on going astray. On your Path, do not ask for miracles. Make yourself the miracle of acceptance, joy, courage and calmness. **When going through angst, keep calm, try to be joyful, as our greatest test is to go beyond the mind, the thoughts, the fears, the logic and the injustice, just have faith in the wisdom, grace and compassion of The One**. It is difficult but this is the Path. Walk it with a smile.'

Baba stood up and they began to explore the village. He played marbles with the children while Rudra sat under another tree and just took in the bliss of the moment. Baba came after a while and joined Rudra.

'You are wondering how to go about all this with calmness when the heart is torn and circumstances are against you? Beta, it starts with the need for peace and the need for peace will make you understand that it is only with a calm mind that you can embrace peace. Calmness is another word for wisdom. Calmness and wisdom are two sides of the same coin. We shall now be blessed with your horrible tea. Come let us go back home.'

In an instant they were back in the cottage. It was afternoon. Rudra put the water to boil and arranged a plate of humble peanuts. Baba liked to snack a little on these strange delicacies of chai and peanuts.

They sat in their semi-dark room with oil lamps
burning and snacked. Rudra lit a chillum for Baba which
Baba smoked and then passed back to Rudra. It was all
done in complete silence. There was no room for words
or thoughts. They just were one with stillness of the
moment. Rudra heard his brood play about outside on
the veranda. Life was good. Life was cool.

*Calmness leads to further stillness. Restlessness leads
to further chaos.*

A FEW DAYS later back on the beach, around three in the morning, Baba sat down and Rudra knew the Old Man would resume the talk from that serene village of stillness.

'Beta, the one who understands the working of Karma is a wise individual. As I have told you before, if you believe in the Goddess, God and Guru, you have to believe in the laws of Karma. There is no other way around. Otherwise you are praying to an unjust Force. The One is never unjust but is the most Just One. If you do not believe in Karma then you might as well not believe in the Goddess, God, and Guru. It is as simple as this. So a wise being, respects the laws of cause and effect; respects the laws of Karma. As you have sown, thus you shall reap. When you understand this philosophy, calmness, maturity, wisdom shall envelop you. But understanding Karma and living it are two different worlds. We all know what Karma is but how many of us go through Karma in a peaceful manner? That is where the secret lies. Knowing Karma and living Karma determine everything, beta. Karma comes about virtually countless times in a day. Free will is how we go through the Karma determined for each one of us. Wisdom comes about in the use of free will of embracing one's lot or Karma. Thus, living Karma in the right way shows one's level of maturity and wisdom.

'Knowledge and intelligence are important but wisdom comes forth in living one's life, embracing one's lot calmly while giving each moment our very best. This leads to further calmness and going within and living each moment in the best possible manner. The moment this happens you become still within and a truly calm individual. You become a less judgemental person. You become a more compassionate being. And when you have gone through the process of self-inquiry and you merge your raw material, which are your strengths, weaknesses and limitations, that you have garnered through self-inquiry with your knowledge of how to accept your Karmic lot, you become an evolved soul. It is as simple or as complicated as this uncomplicated philosophy. As simple or as difficult life becomes for the person who knows how to embrace Karma peacefully giving his or her best or how one fights each Karmic experience. In reality this is one of the foundations of spiritual growth. How does one learn to accept his or her lot? That acceptance shall come about with the conscious or subconscious realization of how to embrace one's Karma, as our lot and our Karma are one and the same thing. **You may know all about Karma but if you are not willing to accept it gracefully then you shall never be able to repose in calm and still waters.** You shall always be using your free will to fight your lot and your Karmic blueprint. I hope your thick head is getting all that I am trying to instill within?'

'Yes, my darling Karmic boss!'

'Good. Sometimes the expressions on your face speak of complete daftness. Anyway, just because somebody knows everything or, to the world, is a very wise individual means nothing if that individual does not know how to embrace one's Karma or one's lot with peace and graceful surrender and calm acceptance, but of course after giving each moment one's very best. This is where free will comes into play, giving each moment our very best. The more we give each moment our very best, inherently we are accepting our lot most gracefully. To give each moment our very best we need to understand the workings of Karma and the power of our own free will. So strangely Karma and free will have to work hand in hand for the individual to grow and to come from a place of calmness and stillness; come from *sthirtha*, which means pure stillness.'

'How does one do that, Baba? Especially when one is going through truly rough times.'

'My defrosted worm, understanding that rough times are a part of the Karmic experience and the only free will one has is how we go through that Karmic experience, this is the key to the answer. When we don't try to fight the experience but live it gracefully we are hastening the end of the Karmic experience. The more we fight it we are prolonging the incident. So a wise person goes through the experience calmly giving his or her best to each moment. Others become fearful, bitter, judgemental, slanderous, weak, lose patience and become negative, thus, create more Karma and further strengthen the Karmic experience prolonging it longer than needed. It all depends now on the individual. Not on the Karmic experience but how we embrace that Karmic experience. It is like when one is unable to sleep, either you create hell for yourself and try to force yourself to sleep or you accept that tonight you might not sleep and go about the night in either prayer, reading a book, or thinking happy thoughts, visualizing beautiful scenarios or get angry, distressed, bitter, negative, impatient, restless and stretch the night . . . in reality the duration of the night shall remain the same . . . but you shall either make it seem never-ending or dawn might just come about because you have made peace with the sleepless situation. Remember, you are not going to sleep. That has been predetermined. How you want to spend the rest of the night is up to you. Karma works in the same manner. You have to go through an experience. How you want to go through the experience will be determined by the individual. You can make it more dreadful or you can go through it with calm acceptance giving your best to each moment. Your calm acceptance, meaning your calm free will, might even allow you to sleep for the rest of the night, but your agitation will not allow you to sleep. It is now your free will that is not allowing you to sleep as the Karmic experience might even be over, but you have started something else with the wrong use of your free will. The long night and Karma are similar. How you want to spend that night will depend on your free will. Staying awake for part or most of the night might be Karmic but how you shall spend that night is up to you and your attitude towards the situation. You want to simplify matters or complicate them, that shall depend completely upon you, beta.'

'We all have to go through such nights. If you are in awareness then each night that you are forced to stay awake, you will still be in a state of calmness. But if you react you will wake everyone up and create disharmony for yourself and others.'

'Baba, what is the easiest way to face Karma?'

'The easiest way of dealing with Karma is looking past your ghastly tea through calm surrender. The easiest way of dealing with Karma is giving your best to each moment irrespective of the circumstances. The best way of dealing with Karma is living each moment in silent surrender to one's Goddess, God and Guru, dedicating each moment at Their feet and trying to make Them happy and proud of you each moment of your existence. All that is needed is selfless love and complete surrender to the realization that you are going through your Karmic experience, your Karmic cleansing and your Goddess, God and Guru know best and if They know best then leave the rest to Them and Their plan with graceful surrender. This is the best way to deal with Karma. If you can live your life like this then no philosophies are needed, no meditation, no prayers, no offerings, nothing is needed as your life has become a philosophy, a prayer, an offering and you are living in a constant state of meditation as you are one with the moment all the time.'

'Remember, beta, when the individual leaves the body and has to be present for judgement, at that time the individual has no right or power to explain or justify his or her thoughts, words and actions. Karma has no logic or justification or emotion. It is the law of cause and effect. You have no say in trying to defend your thoughts, words and deeds. Two plus two adds to four; not five, not three, not nearly four, it's just four. Your Goddess, God, Guru will represent you. Your ancestors will represent you. But you yourself cannot represent your justification for anything. And not just what we did but what also we did not do; not what we said but also what we did not say; all these things come into play. Lord Krishna went hoarse trying to explain to one and all that doing wrong and being a mere observer when wrong is being done, both have their Karmic ramifications. Doing evil and observing evil both will be weighed on the Karmic weighing scale. **No matter how wrong somebody may be, the moment we judge or slander that individual, we have begun a Karmic account with that individual**. What an unnecessary account to open with a person you might not have any link with, in a situation which does not concern you at all, for a reason you in all honesty do not even know the reality of it all. But you have opened a Karmic bond and association with that individual by judging and slandering. What a waste of time, energy and opportunity to grow! Often, Karmic relationships are nothing but thoughts, words and deeds that come forth from ignorance or ego or sheer stupidity. Thus, when Karmic ramification knocks at the door be it out of give and take or sheer ignorance or complete lack of common sense, then go through that experience calmly, seeking strength and wisdom to accept one's lot with grace, wisdom and a sense of humour. You have initiated something, only your Master knows when; and now when the collector of the bill knocks on your door for you to pay the bill; just pay the bill with class and grace. The night to stay awake has come, the impact of Karmic milestones which have to be mandatorily experienced can be gone through or even controlled and the magnitude and intensity can be tapered down by your own free will; by your insistence on going through the experience with calmness and compassion for all involved including yourself, beta. Remember this, the more we gravitate towards the external, the more we react, the more we get agitated, more of Karma shall be created. Not because of any other reason but simply due to the wrong use of free will. Once Karma comes into play, again for lifetimes, sometimes, you might get sucked into this never-ending mire of quicksand. All because you did not use your free will wisely. You have only yourself to blame now.'

'Baba, is it as simple as this?'

'Honestly, beta, it is as simple or as complicated as I have explained to you. Remember, Karma is created by the use of free will, perpetuated by the wrong use of it. It is only free will that starts the Karmic account. It shall necessitate that now only the wise use of free will end that Karmic account. The individual is the creator of his or her hell or heaven. The individual is the creator of his or her destiny, his or her own Karmic journey. It began with the use of free will and now it has to end with the right use of free will or it can perpetuate with the wrong use of free will. Till you do not understand this, even if you shall get out of the quicksand, you might once again jump right back into the mire and this cycle won't end till you decide, enough is enough, now once out of this pit I will go and have a bath in the cool waters of the stream flowing and I will not jump back into the pit of mire and quicksand. That is it. The individual will have to decide. Nobody can decide for the person. It's the use of each one's individual free will. Not even Masters shall get involved as you have to show and indicate whether you have evolved, stayed stagnant or regressed. This, you have to prove without any aid. The best part is every moment is a new beginning in the realm of spirituality and every moment is an opportunity to get out of the Karmic pit or go deeper.'

'However murky the situation, each moment is a new beginning where we can redeem ourselves, one step at a time, and most importantly, no matter how pressing our deeds, we need to constantly be on guard as sometimes one wrong thought, word, or deed can push us back into that pit, maybe even push us back by lifetimes. Fear and anger are two things to avoid. Don't be afraid of your pending Karma; try to calmly cleanse it. Don't be angry with your pending Karmic outcome; calmly face it.'

'Baba, what saddens you regarding all this?'

'When most of us know about Karma, about ramifications of Karma, about life after death, about reincarnation, about not being able to take anything with us after we drop the body, except our Karma, but mankind still behaves as though there is no law governing life. It always saddens me how people believe in the laws of Karma and in reincarnation yet still live a life filled with dark desires, wrong thoughts, words and deeds! This goes against all common sense, logic and justification. Why would most of mankind still go about living a life as though there is no law of Karma, no reincarnation, where an individual at the time of passing over can actually take his or her fame, money and power to the other world? **Why would mankind still live a life where Karma, afterlife and reincarnation are myths is something that has never failed to astound the very heavens, every single day**. This is what saddens me. I can understand if somebody does not understand the laws of cause and effect or does not believe in a Superior Power or does not believe in life after death or does not believe in reincarnation and goes about living a debauched life, goes about living a life of impurity and misconduct. I can understand if for an individual this life is it, and whatever he or she experiences is meant only till the person is in the body and once the person drops the body, that is it. No heaven or hell, no ramifications of thoughts, words and deeds, then I understand the self-centredness and darkness of that individual. But if you profess to believe in the Goddess, God and Guru, when you profess to believe in life after death, when you are certain of the laws of Karma and retribution and of the judgement day, then how dare you live a life which is not, in each moment, trying to move you closer to The One and which is not, in each moment, trying to make

your Goddess, God and Guru happy and proud of you?
This is what I do not understand. How can you pray and
then behave in a mean and petty manner? How can you
chant Mantras and then slander? How can you meditate
and then create havoc and hell in the lives of others? I do
not understand this. If you believe then let your thoughts,
words and actions show your belief. If you do not believe
then it doesn't matter. You shall go through your strife
and your Karmic retribution in this or some other life but
at least you have not lived a life of a hypocrite. You have
lived a life of what you have believed or not believed in.
You haven't believed in God or Karma and you have
lived a life that proves you don't believe in anything
beyond your external life. But don't believe and then go
about living a life of a non-believer. Don't for a moment
say Their Name and then live a life that shows you have
never ever heard about Them. That is not right, beta.
We all know we are going to drop the physical body.
We all know we cannot take anything with us but our
deeds and Karma. We all know there is a law of cause
and effect. Yet look at the lives of most people. It will
convince you that none of them know about anything
other than their petty and external life. This is worrying,
because if you know about spirituality and still live a life
that is exactly opposite to your beliefs then what hope is
there for anybody to learn from example and walk the
Path? What hope is there for that individual? You really
think the sinner and the Saint shall be judged on one
scale? No, beta. You will be judged by who you are and
thus, the fall of a Saint is far steeper and the hell that

awaits is countless times more gruesome than that which waits for somebody who never knew and never believed and never understood. The more we know the steeper is the fall, for after knowing and understanding we still messed up. We have no excuse, we have no justification. **That is why I have told you that Karma decides the playing field. Free will decides how we play it**. If you are aware and do not use your free will in the manner that shows respect to your awareness about life and the beyond then there is something drastically wrong with the individual. If you know that slandering is wrong and you continue to slander, what does that say about you? If you know judging somebody is not right and you continue to judge one and all, what does that say about you? It's all well and good to pray and meditate and be knowledgeable about spirituality but if you cannot talk the talk and walk the walk then you are nothing but a hypocrite or a very weak willed individual. Get your act together. If you are on a Path then walk that Path with respect, give that Path the respect. Either you are spiritual or you are not spiritual. You cannot be spiritual where it is convenient and not spiritual to suit the demands of the moment. Then that person who is completely debauched is better than you as at least that person is not trying to show anybody else any better. He or she knows who he or she is and is living that life. No hypocrisy is involved.'

'Baba, life is tough and we are weak.'

'Beta, the meals dished out in the Karmic kitchen are often unpalatable. That does not mean one has to cut off one's tongue. You just never know, the most sublime delicacy might just be a spoonful away. One cannot stop a raging fire by tackling it with greater fire. Karmic fire can only be doused by calmness and the right use of free will, not by aggression or in a reactive manner. Till you do not understand this simple philosophy, life will always be difficult and tough and mankind shall always feel that it is weak. When in reality mankind is the special one. It is the only species on Mother Earth that can evolve voluntarily and achieve Godhood. Beta, Goddess, God and Guru are not involved in our free will or Karma. This is our individual responsibility. The faster you understand this, the calmer life will become. Karmic ramifications and the Karmic cross can only be made lighter by spreading happiness, taking care of those in dire need, by indulging in charity, by wiping away a tear, by spreading a smile, through prayers, meditation but first and foremost, through positive and graceful surrender to the wisdom of The One. By giving your best to each moment and then embracing whatever is in store with calm surrender and with infinite patience and grace.'

'Beta, there is no other way. Ups and downs are a part of the Karmic cycle. During both times live in awareness. When you are flying high, do not forget that eventually you have to come back to Mother Earth. When you are down and out never forget that Mother Earth is your mother and She loves you and if you let Her, She will protect you in Her warm embrace.'

They stood up and walked on the beach. It was around four thirty in the morning. A few birds flew over their heads and then the duo returned to the cottage.

Baba sat down to pray and indicated to Rudra to sleep for a while. Rudra lay down next to Baba's feet and slept in an instant.

Remember, Karma is created by the use of free will, perpetuated by the wrong use of it. It is only free will that starts a Karmic account. It shall necessitate that now only the wise use of free will end that Karmic account.

RUDRA SAW HIMSELF on the mountain, alone. And all the wrong he had thought, spoken, or done came back to him and it was disgusting. For all his spiritual tendencies and growth he had a long way to climb up the Mountain, he realized. It was unnerving to see every minute flaw within him. The wrongs done were not great in magnitude but were many in number. The words spoken may not have been horrible but they were wrong. The thoughts were not gruesome but they were not meant to have originated from him, though they had, and he carried this cross in the dream and each time he realized that he had done wrong and truly regretted the thought, word or action, the cross got a little lighter. It was strange. It felt as though he was being washed off his sins with the realization of his mistakes. He did not once try to justify any wrongdoing, even though he was tempted to. **As Baba so often said, what is wrong cannot be made right with justification or afterthought. What is right needed no justification or logic**. Rudra climbed this mountain with the cross. There were countless others who made the same climb. All those who tried to justify their wrongdoings slipped or Rudra could make out that their cross got heavier. Nobody was whipping them or tormenting them. It was their individual journey. Rudra often halted to weep and he cried bitterly for all the wrong he had ever thought, spoken or done. By God! He was a sinner, he realized, as he had so often messed up by slandering and judging. Most of the wrong could have so easily been avoided. He had created his own hell. Dug his own pit and for no real reason. Life in the village below went about as normal. He could see smoke come out of the chimneys and he envied those in their homes, surrounded by their loved ones, while here he made this treacherous climb with this huge cross which was now much lighter than when he had begun the journey. He was strangely in no rush to reach the top. He wanted to experience all the pain and the angst. He wanted to weep. He wanted to suffer, as in his suffering was his release. He looked up and saw innumerable ones who now looked healed and their crosses had disappeared or become very small and light. He did not envy them. He was happy for them. He wanted them to be free of their crosses and the moment he had this thought, considerable weight from his own cross disappeared. He realized that the happier he was for others the calmer he felt and the more he was released of his suffering. He realized that those who are happy in the happiness of others are truly blessed children of The One. Jealousy and envy are chains that drag even Giants into the muck of despondency and Karmic ramifications. Something as simple as praying for the happiness of all and truly meaning the prayer, made Rudra feel light in the heart and the weight of the cross reduced dramatically, and praying for the well-being of others made Rudra feel truly happy from within. Rudra now understood the real meaning of freedom. **Being free meant living for others. Being free meant praying for others and being free meant being happy for others. Jealousy and envy were chains that made the soul and the spirit earthbound. They are our greatest nemesis; our true arch-enemies**.

Rudra understood that we originate most of our Karmas without reason or justification. Take jealousy and envy. These two emotions erupt within ourselves when we see others successful or happy or rich or living a life we aspire to live. But as Baba so often said that there are no free meals in the cosmos, which meant if somebody was going through a fabulous time in life, he or she had worked for that kind of life, in this lifetime or in the past. To feel jealous or envious towards the person was so illogical. If we wanted that kind of life, we needed to work for it and in this life or in the next, for sure, we too would live that life. But to be jealous about somebody's success was like sitting at the base of a mountain and hating those who were climbing high and taking in the beautiful scenery and the breathtaking view they could see and capture and the cool air that they breathed in. If we wanted all that we too had to make the climb sometime or the other. Feeling envious or jealous about where they had reached and hoping they would fall or be miserable only made our Karmic blueprint tarnished further.

Rudra looked below and saw many climbers struggle and prayed for them. He had been where they were and he wanted to help them but he couldn't. He truly prayed. They understood that by truly regretting and repenting for the wrongdoings and not repeating them their cross would get lighter and the climb easier. Rudra's cross became exceedingly light. He understood the true meaning of compassion now. Compassion meant feeling exactly what others were going through and wanting to help them go beyond their discomfort.

Rudra continued his climb with the cross now considerably lighter than when he had started. He truly wished that he could tell those below him the secret of climbing faster and making the cross lighter but he couldn't and he also knew they wouldn't understand. They had to learn all this on their own. Allow their free will to help them learn the secret of setting themselves free from base emotions.

Rudra continued to witness all the wrong he had done and began to learn how not to live and how to live. Everything that Baba had taught him came to mind and it was a strange realization that eventually everything was in his control and in his hands. How he decided to live or not live would decide everything concerning him. It was a strange realization that he was truly the master of his own destiny. There was Karma and there was free will and between the two all else would be decided. He continued the climb upwards until he woke up to find Blondie with her head on his stomach, snoring away blissfully. The Sun was already above his head and Baba sat by the window seeing the waves playing their music.

'Why didn't you wake me up, Baba?'

'Oh, I woke you up nice and good, my child, and you were wide awake in your dream learning so much about life and the cross which is all that matters.' Saying this Baba chuckled. Rudra prostrated himself at Baba's feet and then rushed to wash up and put the morning chai to boil.

There was Karma and there was free will and between the two all else would be decided.

THEY WERE IN the cottage. It had suddenly begun to rain. Although monsoons were months away, it had begun to pour and the divine fragrance of the earth was overpowering. They sat on the veranda sipping chai. Rudra had prepared a strange mixture of boiled corn and peanuts and Baba ate a little but with relish. The brood of dogs sat huddled on the side of the veranda enjoying the coolness of the floor but making sure that not a drop of water touched them. One could barely see the ocean due to the rains and it was a heavenly sight. Baba lit the chillum and after a while passed it to Rudra who had a few drags and passed it back to Baba. The sweet taste of the tobacco with the unsweetened chai was a perfect combination.

'Beta, what is wisdom? Don't you dare try and reply, I know your answer which isn't full of wisdom. Wisdom, beta, is the choice one makes to embrace a particular situation and complete wisdom is the choice one makes to embrace each moment. Not knowledge or intellect but wisdom is what is going to decide how an individual is going to meet each moment and how each moment is going to be treated. The individual who is aware of each moment is going to embrace each moment with a particular maturity and grace. The one who is lost to

thoughts and emotions and uncertainties is going to meet
that moment unprepared. The less prepared you are to
welcome each moment, more often than not you are
going to come from indecisiveness and reaction. The
more aware you are, the greater the wisdom with which
you shall embrace each moment. When I say you are
aware or you come from a place of awareness it means
that you are present in each moment. You are not lost to
the moment. You are not lost to thoughts or preoccupied
but you are absorbed with each moment. The time you
are absorbed with each moment you shall rarely come
from reaction but from a place of calmness. You are no
longer a headless chicken. You know exactly what is
going on and what is expected of you and what is the
best that you can give. Your best may not be enough for
the situation or the moment but remember it is your best
and coming from your best you cannot do any better,
and thus, you have given your best to each moment and
nobody in heaven can ask more of you.'

'Wisdom is not about knowledge or information.
Wisdom is when one gives one's best with perfect grace
and calmness and knowing when something is beyond
you, admitting it and seeking guidance for the same.
Wisdom is not about knowing everything. It is just about
giving your best to each moment in the calmest manner
coming from a place of compassion without ego. The
body may thirst for wine but one may truly only need
water. The wise know the difference between their wants
and their needs. The wise know the difference between
their strengths and their weaknesses and limitations. The

wise know when something is doable and when one needs assistance to go through some work. The wise also know that every moment has its own demands and needs. **Sometimes what a piece of chocolate can do for the state of mind and well-being, the scriptures cannot**. The wise have their finger on the pulse of the moment. It is spiritual common sense. You don't need to be well-versed with the scriptures but you need to be completely in the moment to understand what is needed and what is not. Remember, a wise person knows how much to bite and how much can be chewed. Oscillation in our spiritual pursuits very often comes about when we operate from overt eagerness. This comes about as a reactive state and not as a calm proactive state. The wise never come from a reactive state, beta. They know there is no sense in rushing into something. They know there is no sense in trying to hasten a process. Everything when done calmly usually gets completed. When we rush into something we usually land up tripping over our own selves. The wise know this. They are not trying to compete with anybody. The wise know that a wrong doesn't become right by raising one's voice or by being aggressive. In fact, right becomes wrong if expressed to hurt or wound somebody. Sometimes you can be completely right but the way you have gone about trying to prove yourself or the way you have gone about expressing yourself can make you absolutely wrong. Usually when we are right a certain level of ego enters our attitude and speech and tone. That makes us wrong then. So we are right but the way we have gone about it has made us wrong. The wise will admit to their mistakes calmly and humbly and thus, though they may be wrong, the way they have gone about accepting their mistake eventually might make them right about the way the entire process was handled. You can be right ungracefully or you can be gracefully wrong. You can be an egoistic victor or a very graceful loser. What would you prefer to be, beta? An egoistic victor or a graceful loser? Ideally a graceful victor but for that you need to be in the moment calmly. Look around you, you will see so many egoistic victors and you know they are right and that they are victorious but they have left a stench you don't care much about. They have left a bad taste in the mouth. You do not want to emulate them. You don't begrudge them their victory, you just don't want anything to do with them or their victory. And then there are those who have been so graceful in their defeat that you want to embrace them and nurture them. Yes, if you are fortunate you shall find somebody who has won and won with such class that you are left spellbound. Their victory or state of conviction has humbled you. This is how one needs to be in any state of victory. You should gracefully be humble around all. You shouldn't be begrudged by your attitude. **One needs certain poise and acceptance in losing but there should be a greater elegance and humility in winning.'**

'Also, the wise know that fame and popularity are not friends; just loud neighbours one can't do much about. The wise do not get swayed by either. You are famous and popular one day and the next day people are baying for your blood. All you have done is gone about your life and your work. You have no idea why you were famous and now so infamous. The only thing in your hands is to continue going about each moment as calmly as possible. If you are swayed away by pomp and glamour you will be terribly disillusioned then when all of it is taken away. But if your priority is clear and you do not lose sight of your priority then you shall not be distraught or distracted when things don't go or do go your way. The wise know this.'

'Baba, what is the simplest philosophy to follow when out in the world?'

'My toad, do unto others what you would want others to do to you is one of the most underrated spiritual gems of all times. If you can base your life on this philosophy you will go a long distance. Of course, others may not follow this philosophy and the faster you understand this the better, as it shall save you from a lot of heartbreak. But if you are asking me how to move forward on the spiritual path, this is as good a spiritual foundation as any. If you do not like others slandering you, then you should not slander. If you do not like others cheating you, then you should not cheat. If you want others to treat you with respect, you need to start by treating others with respect. Whatever you want others to live by, you should first start living with those same qualities. Yes, very importantly, you should understand that most people are not going to live up to your philosophy but that should not deter you from walking the Path. You will eventually have others treating you the way you treat them. Not everybody but at least a few, which is as good as it gets.'

'Also, beta, those whose lives are dictated by what the world thinks about them or talks about them, are going to get disillusioned for sure. Don't seek validation from the world. It has a tendency to crucify whomever it once loved. When we die, will it matter what people say about us or will our Karmic journey decide our life ahead? Only our thoughts, words and actions are going to decide our lives ahead. Not what people have thought or spoken about us. But yet those who are not wise let others dictate their lives by their opinions and their talks. It is a foolish way to live. The wise do not let this dictate their lives. Dust to dust is a reality most people know about but very few truly understand, and fewer live. Let permanence decide your life. Talk and opinions are transient. Let them not decide your moment-to-moment thoughts, words and deeds. If you know your strengths, weaknesses and limitations; if you know your priorities and you calmly give your best to each moment, leaving the rest gracefully to your Goddess, God and Guru or destiny or the cosmos, son, you can never go wrong and you will not be disillusioned. The world can disillusion you or you can delude yourself, but it is best not to allow either to do so.'

'Baba, if you don't have somebody to guide you, how does one know if you are on the right Path?'

'Beta, if we have to convince others of the validity of an action or decision, it is understandable, but if we have to vehemently justify to ourselves about something,

be it a thought, word, action, decision, then it is best
to pause and truly rethink things over. If you do so
calmly you will for sure come to the right decision. Seek
guidance of the wise but also of those who are your well-
wishers. Eventually you will have to decide and then take
responsibility of your decision. Every single moment, we
can either create a dream or a nightmare, as each moment
we either choose to live or choose to kill the opportunity
to live the right life. Beta, as I have told you before, each
moment is in your control. Live in a state of awareness
and you will live right. Live like a headless chicken, then
your fate is in the hands of everything which is reactive
and a gamble.'

'Life is going to offer you various alternatives and
often no alternatives. It is going to depend on each one
of us how we embrace that moment. We would call
somebody an idiot if we saw him trying to collect water
in a clenched fist rather than cupping water gently in
the palms. And yet, we go about doing the same when
it comes to accepting what life has in store for us. When
you hold your palms open you will be able to hold the
water. When you are calm your palms are figuratively
open for you to accept what life is handing out to you,
calmly and by giving your level best to each moment. We
are all vessels. What we decide to fill ourselves up with
will decide eventually where we will be used. In reality,
all scriptures are about this simple reality. The pot that
carries the Ganges water will be taken to the Temple.
The pot that carries dirty water will reach someplace else.
Decide what you want to be filled up with so that you can

be used for things that matter to you. Our temperament is our barometer of peace and chaos within, or of heaven and hell. It's how we accept internally what life hands out to us. It's not about life; it is about how we accept it. So whatever life hands out to an individual is important for sure, but how one accepts it will decide heaven and hell for that individual.'

'The calmer we are, the more we shall fill ourselves up with the right ingredients and the right raw materials, life will work on us with whatever raw materials we hand to the greater force. Give it dirt, it shall create sewage. Give it purity, it shall create nectar. But first one needs to empty oneself of all dirt and baggage. The way forward sometimes begins by clearing the backlog. Sometimes, one needs to take a step back in order to leap ahead. So first empty yourself of all that you need to let go off and then fill yourself up with whatever you need to be filled with. The problem is, we go on living as though this is it, although we know, that all this needs to be released or, it is temporary. The permanent stuff is on a larger level neglected or shoved under the rug. We believe in God, life after death, reincarnation and Karma, but as I have told you, our lives are not led with such understanding. We live in a manner that life is transient. We are aware that in a blink of an eye, destiny and intentions can change, but we go about living life with eyes shut. Thus, being in the moment and living with awareness is the foundation to move ahead and climb the mountain with a cross that is as light as it can possibly be. However noble your intent may be, if not backed by right action, it is like a very strategically dug well, filled with sludge and murky water. I have told you this countless times. **Remember, intention if not backed by the right thoughts, words and deeds lead to nowhere**.'

Suddenly lightning struck deep into the ocean. The intensity of the rain increased. Rudra went into the cottage, got a shawl and placed it around Baba. He went into the kitchen and put water to boil and coal to heat. After the tea was made he offered the cup to Baba who made a face but with a twinkle in His eyes savoured the hot chai. They smoked a chillum and sat looking at the rain, listening to the waves, to the wind's play with the trees. Life was good. Life was cool.

If you do not like others slandering you, then you should not slander. If you do not like others cheating you, then you should not cheat. If you want others to treat you with respect, you need to start by treating others with respect.

RUDRA WAS BACK on the mountain with the cross. This time he saw all the incidents where he was right, but he had handled the situation wrongly, with ego, with condescension, with aggressiveness, with harshness and a sharp tongue, with uncaring attitude; and Rudra cringed. Those around him looked at him with compassion. They too were going through similar experiences. Rudra halted and shut his eyes. How wrong had he behaved when he was right! How many had he hurt with his truth? He realized that he had broken countless hearts with his words and actions and with his way of going about the situation. There was no compassion. There was no tenderness. Just because he was right he had taken the liberty to be petty, mean and offensive. Who had given him this right? He wondered. How could he have behaved so heartlessly? He sat down and wept for the innumerable hearts he had broken. He wanted to go to each of them, touch their feet and seek forgiveness. What a monster he had been! He had done all this repeatedly and that too not in the distant past. As recently as a few weeks ago in channelling, he had hurt a couple with his words. Yes, he was angry at their behaviour, but what right did that give him to behave so callously? Rudra began to cry. He wept with a force that shocked him.

It was for all the good people whom he had hurt because he was right and now he could do nothing to take back his words or his attitude. It was a shameful way of behaving. He pledged never to do this ever again. Whether he was in the right or not, he would never lose his control or conduct himself like this. There wasn't a right in the world that could justify such wrong conduct. It was shameless and uncalled for. He wept more till tears no longer flowed but he wanted to cry more. After a long time he stood up and breathed in deeply. Yes, the cross had got considerably lighter but not his heart. He would never be able to undo the wrong or the hurt he had caused, even if the cross disappeared, his reality would not change. He had hurt innocent people just because he had been right. Never ever would he behave in such a cold-hearted manner!

There isn't a right in the world that can justify
wrong conduct.

THE NEXT FEW days Rudra channelled for innumerable people as Baba had left, to return soon. Rudra had not got over the experience on the mountain yet and it hurt him tremendously knowing he had broken so many hearts with his words. He called up as many people as he could and apologized to them, but most of them did not remember or were kind enough to pretend that they did not recollect the incidents. For lunch he ate at Martins' and dinner was with his brood, usually something he had packed from Martins'. He had tea with a simple snack. He missed Baba a lot and those days he spent more time with Blondie and the rest of the gang. Baba returned after three days and He seemed tired. For the next two days Rudra did nothing but take care of Baba and His fatigued body. He never ever asked Baba any question about his travels, as and when, and if Baba wanted to reveal He would and Rudra would hear all, transfixed.

They were back on the beach. The sky was clear and the stars shone luminously. The sea sparkled. The waves sang their melodious song. It was around two thirty in the morning. Baba and Rudra sat on the cool sand while the brood played about closely on the wet beach. They ran and entered the water and frolicked and ran back to the dry sand and shook the water off and once again they ran back to the water.

'Baba, what is most important on this journey?'

'Gratitude and compassion are most important, beta. You need to be in a constant state of gratitude no matter how difficult the Path or the circumstances. Things can always be slightly worse. The road can also be a little more treacherous and slippery. Thus, always be in a state of gratitude and walk the Path with complete compassion for one and all, including oneself. When you are in a state of awareness then no matter what, you are protected; it makes every step a blessing on the way back Home. To be able to relish what one has, no matter how humble, is a gift you give yourself. To be able to forget or let go of pain, angst or what one will never have is sheer grace, a gift from the cosmos, which you receive when you are in a state of gratitude. Remember a glow-worm might never be able to grasp the vastness and the power of the Sun but all it needs to do is happily glow and be content in its own radiance, which means each of us have to be content with our lot and be happy with whatever our lot is, this is sheer grace. Gratitude and humility come forth from the certainty that all good that flows from each one of us is only and solely because of Grace and when you live a life with such a sublime philosophy, life becomes beautiful, even Divine.

'My glow-worm, let us take an individual who has reasonable health, a semblance of family life, a roof to sleep under, food on the table, clothes to wear, and yet that individual is miserable, God help that person if true misfortune pays a visit. But when one is in a state of gratitude for the little blessings then the ability to face true misfortune comes naturally to such a person. The path of gratitude is the true Path. Yes, life can be painful but a life of gratitude is the only road where our love for The One is not only truly tested but weighed, measured and clothed, not by The One but by our own higher self. When you insist on living in a state of gratitude, the darker the room, the more brilliant shall be the flame that shines forth from the humble oil lamp. Sometimes, one has to be bathed with the cold strife of discomfort to appreciate the warmth of normalcy and whatever little one may possess, but if you live always seeking more, then you fail to appreciate what you have and are blessed with. That is why, My son, if one is content with one's lot, however humble that lot may be, it is one of the pillars of spirituality and the cornerstone of happiness. Thus, for me, to live in a state of humility filled with compassion and joyous gratitude are the foundations of all that which is spiritual. **If you are in a state of gratitude you will naturally be filled with humility and compassion. If you are filled with compassion you shall have gratitude and humility as your companions**. Then however much one earns, lots or meagre, wherever one lives, in a mansion or in a hut, all will be embraced as a blessing, without condescension or want, with sheer graceful joyous acceptance. Be in the moment, in awareness, and you shall not lose your way. The person who decides to find flaws in everything, for him or her even heaven will be left wanting and if one decides to accept all in gratitude, even hell will be a profound learning experience. Sometimes, one's entire life, spirituality and philosophy, can be summed up in one's attitude of whether the glass is half empty or half full. The former indicates playing the victim and thus, being in perpetual discomfort and want, while the latter is living a life of grace in sheer gratitude to each moment. Nothing shall change but one's attitude towards each moment. Remember, even the loftiest of eagles have to swoop down for sustenance and survival. The wise are aware of this and always have their heads held high, but with feet firmly on the ground.'

'Baba, but very often the individual goes through real strife. Take ill-health of oneself or one's loved ones.'

'Yes, beta, it is all a part of the Karmic experience. If the body is your be-all and end-all of everything and not the spirit and energy within you then ill-health cripples not only the body but often the mind and one's very essence. It can make you bitter. It can break you down. Only those immersed in gratitude come out unscathed. Only those who have accepted their lot with calm and even joyous surrender to the divine plan and the divinity of the laws of Karma and continue to give their best to the moment, experience true freedom and liberation. What is this state of being in gratitude, beta? It is when an individual is always in a state of thanks to each moment. We call this state the state of being in *shukar*. What does living in a state of shukar mean? It means that you are thankful for everything and you are thankful and in gratitude for everything. Good or not so good, harsh or pleasant, wealth or poverty, you are in a state of thankful gratitude.'

'Being in a state of gratitude or being in a state of shukar is the most sublime display of love for The One. The one who lives in a constant state of gratitude humbles the very heaven itself. But how many of us, beta, live in a state of gratitude and shukar no matter what is going on externally or internally in our lives? What is shukar? Thanking The One for the food we eat, the water we drink, the clothes we wear, our health and well-being and of our loved ones, constantly, this is living in a state of shukar. Thanking The One for simple joys and sweet happiness in our lives is shukar. To be thankful for all that we have is being in a state of gratitude and shukar for sure, and many live such a life. The real test of shukar is when you are truly thankful even when things are not going according to your plan. That is really living in a state of gratitude and shukar. When we are getting a pounding of our lives and still we can live in the state of gratitude then we are truly living in a state of shukar. This state of gratitude requires us to be thankful even when nothing is going as planned or desired. When everything is going wrong, as though living a nightmare and you can still live in a state of gratitude then, my sweet, crazy child, you are living in a state of shukar. When the worst fears are being realized and you are still in a state of gratitude then you are truly living a life that The One is proud of.'

'It is all fine when things are going as planned and we are in a state of gratitude but the true spirit of gratitude comes forth when things aren't going as planned.

Everything is going downhill with ferocious intensity. When one is going through the worst phase of one's life and one can still be in a state of gratitude then that is the true sign of spirituality and love for The One. See the lives of all the true Masters and those who are firm on the spiritual path, they have all shown gratitude during adversity and trials and tribulations, not only to teach us mere mortals that this is the true way on the Path and the most genuine way of loving your Goddess, God and Guru, but also to tell us that no matter what, being in a state of shukar is the only true way of surrender and faith, and the most profound way to express our love for The One.'

'Baba, there are many who are at least in a state of gratitude when things are going right. Is that not better than always being in a state of greed?'

'Of course, idiot child of mine, it is better to be in a state of gratitude than to be in a state of perpetual want and greed, but how many are truly in a state of shukar even when things are going right, being in a state of true gratitude and thanks? Most are scared that if they aren't in a state of gratitude then the blessed thing might be taken away from them, thus they are in gratitude due to fright and fear. So many are in gratitude simply because of fear of loss or fear the wrath of The One if they were not in a state of gratitude even after having their way. How many truly feel gratitude? If you felt gratitude it would show in your conduct. It would make you more compassionate, more giving, more caring and tender. How many truly change for the better when things are going their way? Very few truly change for the better, beta.'

'When those who are spiritual and walking the spiritual path, go through strife, their love for The One is never questioned. They don't look heavenward and question The One, 'Why me?' They don't try to analyse as to why, after all, their spirituality and good deeds and moral code of decency, are they still getting their noses rubbed into the ground. They go about their lives never once questioning the love of The One. They don't get bitter or negative. They don't get despondent for long. There is no place for anger, bitterness, negativity and hatred for those on the true Path. They will never play the victim card as they are still in the state of shukar. They are certain, assured, convinced and in peace with the knowledge that their Goddess, God and Guru, know what is best for them and their loved ones and as The One knows what is best for each one of them, then why grieve or get agitated or question the fact that He or She knows best and if They know best then all is well. There is no place for anger, bitterness or negativity.'

'Shukar is the faith that resides in the breath of all those who are truly brave enough to enter hell for a heavenly cause and enter heaven not because of any other reason but because that is where The One resides. If The One were to go to hell the true disciples would follow The One into hell as "wherever Thou resides, oh Fulgent One, I shall come along with You as my place is only with You." So, my child, living in a state of gratitude or living in a state of shukar is so sublime a state of living that even the very Gods aspire for it. Let us not be thankful for just a few things going our way but for everything going either our way or not going anywhere. Even when you are being flogged and are bruised and bleeding, all you do is smile and whisper "*shukar*."'

'Baba, you speak very highly about compassion. What is compassion?'

'My sweet, melancholy child, compassion is in reality nothing but Oneness. When you feel the pain and angst of another and you want to help erase that pain—that is compassion. When you want to wipe the tears of somebody and fill the person with joy—that is compassion. When you want all of creation to sleep with a full belly—that is compassion, even if it means you can only help a few to go beyond hunger. Compassion is what prevents the destruction of the world and allows a humble flower to spread its fragrance. It is the root cause of all existence and the reason why Mother Earth revolves around the Radiant Sun. It is the end-all and be-all of things. Now don't you pretend that you have fallen asleep, you rascal!'

'Baba, explain to me because I can barely understand anything . . .'

'That is how I always explain everything to you, you worm. Let me rephrase and further simplify it for you, but now we shall return to our cottage. We will resume this talk tomorrow when your head is ready to absorb more of what I say to you.'

They stood up and walked back to the cottage. The brood followed. Rudra put the water to boil and a piece of coal to heat. It was a little cold outside but the cottage was nice and warm. Baba sat for prayers and after they drank their chai and smoked their chillum, Baba resumed His prayers while Rudra sat nearby and gazed at the sea outside. Life was good. Life was cool.

Being in a state of gratitude or being in a state of shukar is the most sublime display of love for The One. The person who lives in a constant state of gratitude humbles the very heaven itself.

BABA CLIMBED AHEAD while Rudra followed on the mountain, until they reached a village and Rudra could see the various forms of gratitude or the lack of it at play. He saw those who were in a real state of shukar and now he understood what Baba was trying to tell him. Gratitude cannot be faked. You either feel it or you don't. It is either present or absent. You can feign other emotions but never true gratitude as, if you are filled with shukar then naturally each thought, word and action spreads that sublime fragrance. He could see it as clear as day when somebody was filled with true gratitude; it was palpable. It shone through. It was humbling. There were many going through different and difficult experiences, and each of those in real gratitude had a similar fragrance to their very being. It was magical. It was like a symphony in motion. They all went about their lives with a serene calmness, a sense of joy, even though externally or internally they were undergoing hardships or even taking a beating of their lives. Patience and softness exuded from them. You can't feign this. It is either present or not, as simple or as complicated as that. Those who were trying hard to be in that state exuded their own fragrance. Not that they were being untrue or being hypocritical. No. Even those who tried to live in a state of gratitude were on the Path.

It was to their credit that though it may not have come naturally they were striving to walk the Path. But those who understood the philosophy of giving one's best to each moment and leaving the rest to The One joyously, knowing that The One knew best, oh, they shone forth with a different kind of radiance! Rudra was so humbled by these people that he wanted to go and touch their feet. To be able to go through life with a smile and filled with gratitude for all that they were going through, no matter how difficult, is akin to walking through hell for a heavenly cause. So noble, so beautiful, so perfect, like the very heaven itself!

Even Gods were not known to be in a constant state of shukar, which Rudra was certain of. Not that these individuals were perfect. No. They were far from perfect but they were perfect in their imperfections all because of the way they embraced each moment and every circumstance. 'May Baba's blessings be with these people granting them strength and wisdom and may they always live in this state of shukar and gratitude for eternity,' Rudra prayed and then he woke up with Blondie licking his toe. The sun was about to rise and Rudra turned to see Baba sitting still in prayer. He prostrated himself at Baba's feet and after receiving Baba's blessings went to wash up and prepare chai and something for Baba to nibble on.

Gratitude cannot be faked. You either feel it or you don't. It is either present or absent. You can feign other emotions but never true gratitude as, if you are filled with shukar then naturally each thought, word and action spreads that sublime fragrance.

THEY WERE IN the cottage. It was nearing midnight. Baba, as usual, began prayers at midnight. He prayed for a while and Rudra prepared chai and heated the coal for the chillum till then. After they had drunk the tea and smoked the chillum Baba looked at Rudra and smiled.

'I had told you that Karmic ramifications and the Karmic cross can only be made lighter by spreading happiness, taking care of those in dire need, by indulging in charity, by wiping a tear, spreading a smile, through prayers, meditation but most of all, through positive and graceful surrender to the wisdom of The One, all done through the grace of compassion. My child, you look as knowledgeable and perceptive as that wooden table in the corner of the room. Let me explain to you in a language that you will understand. First and foremost, always understand that the fragrance you spread with your love and compassion to all fellow beings is the work of God. You may be the medium from which the fragrance spreads but the doer is The One. Shakti never comes from us but always through us. Shakti, The Goddess Energy, comes forth only from The Goddess and fragrances like selfless love and compassion thus come forth from Her. The more you want to spread such divine fragrance, the more you shall be filled with them. The more you are in the state of awareness of spreading selfless love and compassion, The Goddess shall come forth from you in a stronger manner. A simple act of giving makes The One and all the Masters and the Angels ecstatic. So, there must be something very profound, something very spiritual and something very pure in the noble act of selfless giving. You have the heaven applauding and showering blessings and prayers on the one who gives selflessly. So whenever you have the opportunity of giving, beta, give with open arms. You have no idea the favour you are doing to your own self and to your loved ones. Yes, there is a certain grace in giving silently, which only those who come forth from true humility are aware of. Thus, you can give and then you can give silently. Giving itself is a beautiful act, no matter whether you make a song and dance about it or not. Then when you give silently there is a greater fragrance to the power of giving. I have told you time and again that there is a very thin line between philanthropy and self-gratification but how does that matter? Just keep giving.'

'So, Baba, is there a difference between charity and compassion?'

'Yes, my nauseating child. **In charity you give. In compassion you share**. Charity may be indulged in due to a reason or several reasons. Some do so because they have promised their Goddess, God and Guru that if something takes place, or if a project is successful, or if their loved one gets well, or if the child passes with honour, they will feed so many people, clothe that many people, do this and do that. You are charitable for the peace of your ancestors or for the health of your loved ones or for your protection. There are various reasons why an individual may resort to charity. Usually there is a *quid pro quo* involved. Either you want something or something has transpired and it's like a thank you to The One, or a request or even a bribe. That is fine. There is no wrong reason to be charitable. All reasons are valid and good and justifiable. But where compassion is concerned there is only one reason. You cannot bear to see people go hungry. You want to feed them so that at least for a while they do not go hungry. You cannot bear to see people shivering in the cold. You distribute warm clothes and blankets so that they can sleep more peacefully and in the warmth of whatever covers them. You cannot bear to see people ill, so you want to take care of them via medicines and medical help. In compassion there is only one reason, you want to help those people deal with whatever it is that they are grappling with. You are not doing it to please your Goddess, God or Guru and you are not seeking anything or not thanking The One. You want to share whatever you can in trying to take care of those who are downtrodden and cannot provide for themselves. You have no other reason. If you sit to eat and see somebody hungry, you either share your food with that person or you order food for that person. You don't do this because of Goddess, God, Guru; The One is not involved in this process. You are not seeking anything. **Thus, in charity you give while in compassion you share**. In charity there could be an agenda or no agenda. You might want blessings, you might want your work to be done. You might want this or that. But in compassion all you want is that person to not go hungry, be ill or feel the cold. You are not seeking anything else. You are doing so because you can feel that person's discomfort, angst, hunger, cold and illness.

'Now, in charity, if you are seeking blessings from the person whom you are helping, the chances of a Karmic bond taking birth are immense. You give something to seek something—that is the birth of a Karmic relationship. But when you come forth from compassion you are not interested in anything from that individual. In fact, that individual is doing you a favour by allowing you to serve him or her because within you is the need to only serve.

'It is all about being able to feed the hungry, to clothe the naked, to heal the ill, to help those down and out, and all of us can do the above in our own humble way. If everybody was compassionate the have-nots would not exist as the haves would not allow the have-nots to live in penury. If each individual were to share a bit of what he or she has, trust me the have-nots would not be there. Only a tree on the side of a road knows the importance of the morning dew. Sometimes, a little help to those in need can make an unimaginable difference. Thus, always give no matter how little it may seem. Still, just give. Very often you don't even need to give anything tangible but just a kind word, a smile, the right encouragement, can be as important as material aid. When an individual is down and out, a little time spent with that person can be an act of compassion and the greatest of all acts of charity, as, who knows, without those words, that individual could go about causing harm to himself or herself or to somebody else in a fit of anger, depression or frustration. When we uplift somebody who is without hope, either through word, deed or any kind of assistance, we make the heaven glow brighter and the spiritual scriptures worth their wisdom. Our appreciation or encouragement could change a person's life. Imagine the power of words. It can create or destroy. The power to heal comes from the heart that flows with compassion. Do you know what the greatest miracle is, beta? Leading an individual from darkness into light is the greatest of all miracles, as everything noble and good begins when an individual starts embracing the Divine Light and walks the path of radiance. This is compassion of the highest order. Similarly, failure that makes one a more compassionate human being is far greater than success that makes the individual full of himself or herself. Sometimes we need to feel the pain to become more compassionate. Maybe the cosmos has no other way to make us more compassionate than by making us experience hunger, pain, sorrow, loss and anguish. The wise learn from these experiences and become more understanding. Pain opens the door to compassion and love for all of creation and this unlocks the door to paradise and God consciousness. Others waste the opportunity and become negative. So, at every turn you have the power to become compassionate or self-centred. Once again we come back to free will deciding through the Karmic experience, whether we shall embrace heaven, hell or the in-between.'

'Baba, I have seen people giving in a very crude manner. Is it not better not to give than to give in a manner to make the receiver feel inferior and useless about himself or herself?'

'Beta, that is the difference between charity and coming from compassion and I have seen people refusing to give with such humility that it softens the heart and have seen people give in a manner that shrivels the very soul. That is why I told you earlier that there is a certain grace in giving silently, which only those who come with true humility know about. They give in a manner that makes the receiver feel united with the giver. There is no favour in giving and no obligation in receiving. It is done gracefully. As though everything belongs to The One, somebody is only sharing what belongs only to The One, thus, there is no give and take but just sharing. That kind of sharing comes from true compassion. Remember, you cannot take advantage of a person who is compassionate. The person who is compassionate is not trying to prove a point or tick a box or gain anything. He or she gives to share and that person will share only with those who are truly in need as the person has limited means to share. He or she wants his or her limited means to reach the most deserving. In charity you might give to one and all so as to complete the act of charity, but in compassion you will take pains to share your limited means, beta, as it's not just an act, it's your very being.

Remember, beta, compassion is not a formality, it is who you are. It is not something to be done but something that you live by. You can never go wrong when you come from compassion as you are not trying to prove a point or achieve something but you are just being who you are. If somebody cheats you it is that person's issue not yours as you have come from what you thought was right or needed at that particular point. You are just being yourself and when you are yourself you can never be disillusioned. You are not in the act of giving but in the art of sharing. Compassion means spirituality which means to operate from the Spirit. If you operate from the spirit, you operate from Oneness, and if you operate from Oneness, you can never go wrong. Spiritual pursuits or compassion is not something that you just perform. It is one's very reason for existence. Something one doesn't just do, but what one lives for and eventually becomes. It is not something to be over and done with, like an act of charity, but it is a state that we should be in each waking moment of our lives. We come from the philosophy that every soul, every being is sacred, the *atma* being a part of the *Paramatma,* only the level of awareness and realization vary. In compassion, as in spirituality, what one does is far more important than what one can do, or what one wants to do. Walking the Path takes us home. Nothing else will. So, just keep walking.'

Baba then shut His eyes and got into prayers. Rudra sat down and prepared the list of people he had to meet over the next few days. After completing the list he sat in

prayer too and woke up at dawn with Baba still seated in
prayer, having barely moved at all.

Shakti never comes from us but always through us.
When we uplift somebody who is without hope, either through
word, deed or any kind of assistance, we make the heaven glow
brighter and the spiritual scriptures worth their wisdom.

'BABA, WHEN WE indulge in compassion and charity or anything spiritual, what are the things we have to be careful about or avoid?' Rudra inquired while they sat on the veranda of the cottage. It was early in the morning, around three thirty. They had just finished having chai and some toast and were smoking the chillum.

Baba looked into the darkness out at the sea which beckoned with the music of her waves. The moon was hidden behind large clouds and the night enveloped everything around them.

'Beta, very often on the path of spirituality we tend to create more obstacles for ourselves than all the past life Karmas and the movement of planets can conjure. Mankind has an infinite aptitude and an inherent tendency to create problems for itself. Some of the best work in self-destruction comes forth when one is on the path of spirituality. Very often people think they are moving higher and higher on the Path, when in reality spiritual rot has set in and threatens to cover the Divine Spark within each of those individuals. Unfortunately, those who are on this path of creating hurdles for themselves assume that they are superior, blessed, fortunate or more evolved than all those around them or those who are trying to make them see the reality or help them back on the road to a humble spiritual life.'

'The first pitfall on the path of spirituality is ego. Ego is not about personality or individuality but about the refusal to see the inherent truth about oneself. When a person refuses to acknowledge the sludge within; when an individual refuses to keep an open mind; when an individual is under an illusion that only what he or she thinks, says or does is right and everybody else is wrong, spiritual rot sets in, fast and murky. Everybody has an ego. The drive to push an individual to work harder and go beyond one's comfort zone or to strive to become the best or a better human being is not ego, it is one's journey, but when one refuses to be open to listen and learn, that is when false ego has set in and then one's spiritual pace gets a setback and our vehicle starts going in the reverse direction, but the ego has blinded us and we mistake the motion of the vehicle as moving forward when in reality it is moving backwards.'

'One of the main qualities of a sage or an evolved person is humility. You will see them interact with a child and a scholar with the same sense of humility and lack of ego. He or She is like a child eager to learn and never assumes that He or She has all the answers or that the other person's point of view is baseless. When an individual comes forth only as the dust under the Feet of his or her Goddess, God and Guru, and comes forth only as a disciple, having no personal agenda or even individuality, then growth is assured and self-destruction is kept at bay. The spiritual journey continues beautifully.

But the moment an individual assumes that he or she knows everything or is always right, then rot sets in and the individual's spiritual evolution halts.

'Unfortunately, nowadays, even humility has become a badge one wears proudly and thus even humility can often become akin to ego by default when an individual becomes proud of his or her own humility. Humility should be one's inherent tendency rather than some medal that one wears on the chest. That is why the Bible has mentioned that Heaven is filled with children. It does not mean that Heaven is some pre-nursery crèche or school where only children are allowed, but what Lord Christ meant was that only if you are childlike, open to learning even through your mistakes then Heaven is yours for the taking.

'Beta, when you are on the spiritual journey, when you are moving on the Path, your energy or Kundalini Shakti shall rise and with that rise so shall your propensity for pride. You shall get visions, have experiences, avail prophesies, and feel more powerful as you are swimming in the ocean of Oneness. The time spent in prayer, meditation and charity, slowly makes an individual feel that he or she is superior to others. This might happen consciously or unknowingly. This feeling of being special comes to everybody. Either special to one's Goddess, God and Guru or inherently special, as the understanding is that it is only if one is special can they experience all the things which one has begun to experience on the path of prayer, meditation, healing, prophesy and charity. The moment that happens and one refuses to see the rot which has set in or ignore the stench of spiritual deterioration, one's spiritual journey has taken speed but in the reverse direction.'

'That is why so many on the spiritual path go wayward. They go wrong. They change and become less of who they were. They lead themselves and their followers in the erroneous direction. The more spiritual you are, the more followers you will have. But having followers is nothing to be proud of. It comes with great responsibility. Hitler and despots have had followers too, so why will spiritual leaders or those on the path of spirituality not have followers? Some might have a handful and some may have countless followers, but even if one person is following you, owing to your spiritual growth and you lead that person down a dark alley, the wrong Karma you shall build up is colossal. There is a special hell, far more gruesome than the normal one, described by the learned, reserved for those who in the name of the Goddess, God and Guru spiritually mislead anybody, even a single person seeking refuge from their plight, ignorance or hardships.

'The ego is the quicksand for all spiritual seekers and leaders. The Path is filled with landmines. The landmines are so well hidden that even those who are very evolved sometimes forget where the landmines are buried.'

'Baba, why does the ego set in when on the path of spirituality? Shouldn't, in fact, ego be diminished and humility reign?'

'Yes, my fruitcake of a child, but ego sets in because the individual begins to think that he or she is special, and worse that he or she is the doer and not a vessel for goodness to flow. The moment you think you are the doer, ego sets in. The moment you think you are praying, you are healing, you are channelling, you are providing, you are giving charity, you are compassionate and humble, ego sets in. Till you are certain that you are the vehicle through which all is taking place, you are safe. Till you believe yourself to be just a vessel, a medium, an instrument, you are safe. The moment you believe you are the doer, you are the one and you are special, ego and spiritual decline set in. Yes, for sure you have to give your best to each moment, but when you believe that it is you who is doing things, thinking things, saying things, curing and performing miracles, then your downfall commences and in a blink of an eye, in reality, you are in quicksand when according to you, you are soaring with the Angels. When you give your best but with the firm realization that it is only through Their Grace that everything noble and good takes place and we have the good fortune of being blessed that something good comes forth from simple folks like us and that we are only instruments for Their Glory to shine through, we are secure in Their love and protection. Thus, it is mandatory and crucial that we remind ourselves countless times a day, in fact, best would be if we never forget even for a single moment, that we are mere mediums or instruments for Their music to flow through, be it in the big things of life or in the humblest moments. When we go about each moment in gratitude and humility, it is then that our spiritual journey catches speed and we truly begin to climb that elusive mountain. **When we watch**

each thought, word, action, as an observer, we will see how often our ego is at play and it never fails to astound me as to how easily we forget the simple rule that "I am not the doer, I am the instrument through which all good and noble from The One flows through." Humility is the cloak that shields us from our own self-destructiveness on this Path. It shields, nurtures, enhances and speeds up the pace, ensuring that we shall never fall off the seat. Humility is so underrated, so out of grace with most people that it is little wonder that there are very few who truly practise it. It is for each one to go within and find out whether we operate from ego or as the dust beneath the Feet of our Goddess, God and Guru. Do we come forth as the doer or as the humble flute from which flows Their divine and ecstatic music?'

'Mercy, Baba, on us all is all I can pray for now.'

'Ah! My boy, what a beautiful word you have uttered. Mercy. *Reham*. The word Mercy or Reham if chanted with selfless purity through the day itself will make you reach the very doorsteps of Heaven. Shukar will get you in but to reach the gateway of Heaven, this humble word, Reham, will do the needful. You see, son, as I have told you now, most people are losing sight of the larger picture by losing the very essence of spirituality, which in reality resides in the humblest of all wombs and all things. For instance, we no longer sit silently and just observe our breath enter our body, move within and then leave ourselves. It is the simplest of all spiritual practices, the most ancient one, which has led many on the Path and has shown either glimpses or the entire blueprint of the Big Plan. It is no longer enough to sit silently anywhere and just be and become one with the breath. The old-fashioned way of just being and sitting silently or even lying down and becoming one with the breath is considered redundant. Now it is all about some technique or about chakras or Kundalini or something or the other. Reham too seems to have become an old-fashioned way. Not enough for most. Mercy or pity is considered as the sign of losers now, not of strength. Look at it this way, often we are so self-destructive that only Divine Pity or Divine Mercy can save us from digging our graves deeper into the bowels of hell, chaos and insanity, but will we ask for Mercy or Reham? No, we will seek other things but not this most humble of all prayers and wishes.'

'All that we go through is the ramification of our thoughts, words and deeds, either from the past lifetime or from past lifetimes. So, when we say, have mercy on me, it doesn't only mean forgive me; it means tender Your justice with compassion. If I have to lift a thousand bricks, don't let me lift them in one attempt, it shall break my back. Let me lift the load, maybe a few at a time, as I know that it is the burden of my stupidity and I shall bear the burden, but have mercy on me, oh Merciful One, as I know I have wronged but have mercy on me. My child with the intellect of a shoe lace, are you understanding me?'

'Oh yes, my Cobbler King.'

'Rascal. So, when we use a simple word like Reham, coming from the depths of our very being and we truly mean it, what we are telling the Fakir is that don't let go of my hand, however difficult I make it for You. Reham is a word that can make the very heavens more compassionate when it comes from the depths of your true within. For me it is one of the most powerful words ever scripted. It is a word in reality not scripted by mankind but by the very Angels Themselves. Which other words do you think are scripted by the Angels, my daft child?'

'Cash please. Instant downloading . . .'

'*Ya Khuda!*' sighed Baba with a smile and a twinkle in His eyes. 'When one calls out Reham from the depths of one's very being, the words leave from one's soul and reach the Feet of our Goddess, God and Guru. When we bless somebody *Allah Reham Karay*, we are blessing the individual that may the Almighty have compassion on you and give you the strength and wisdom to go through the experience with calmness and grace. Like when I have your tea I always whisper Reham so that I can gulp your tea without wincing.'

'So hilarious, my Lord and Master.'

'Not like you who cusses like a dehydrated sailor when Martins' food is not to your liking. Anyway, we need to incorporate this one word into our very being. I love this word Reham as it makes each one of us a child pleading for an understanding and another chance from our Elders. You reflect on this word and it opens doors deep within your heart that have been shut for a long time, sometimes for a number of lifetimes. When you meditate on this word it makes everything so sublime and simple. Take your Goddess, God and Guru's name and then add Reham to it. Inhale, mentally chanting your Goddess, God and Guru's name and exhale, mentally chanting Reham. Let the energy of the Divine enter with every inhalation and let the word Reham exhale all your angst and burdens. We are seeking forgiveness not only from all of creation but from ourselves too. As very often we are our greatest enemies as we make ourselves go through all the angst and pain, through all the filth which we cover ourselves with through our thoughts, words and deeds. When we seek mercy, we are telling Them that whatever has been done, wherever it has been done, whenever it has been done, to whomever it has been done, however it has been done, have mercy on me. You can seek forgiveness but forgiveness comes with a clause. One seeks forgiveness and then strives never to repeat the same mistake for which one is seeking forgiveness from. But most of us seek forgiveness and then like good buffoons we amazingly repeat the same blunder again and again. To seek forgiveness means that we shall try our best not to repeat that blunder but so often that is not the case. But Reham on the other hand means, "Oh my Creator, I am daft, dumb and weak, have compassion on me, have mercy on me, have pity on me, as no matter what, I might again make mistakes but You never stop having mercy and pity on me." So, one is seeking mercy not only from one's flaws and all the muck but also seeking Reham from one's own self-destructive nature. This allows grace to embrace us. But this works when you seek mercy from the very depths of your being. It's not a word, it's a way of life.'

'Only when one keeps seeking Reham and we truly mean it, then slowly we too begin to get more compassionate and forgiving to one's own self and all those around us. When we have our head at the feet of The One and seek Reham and truly seek it, grace descends, it has to. Our issues may remain but a certain resolve, a certain calmness enters us and our very being and all the noise within us dissolves into nothingness and we begin to be more compassionate and forgiving to others too. Our real issue is that we are low on Reham, we need to fill ourselves up with Reham.'

'Reham, this simple word can change the way we see and live life, see the world and the beyond. We come from The One. The One embodies our Divine Mother and Divine Father. Both rolled into One; *Shiv Shakti*, Ahura, Allah, God. Rules abide. Karma seeks its pound of flesh. But there are certain cards held by The One, the card of compassion, mercy, pity. Call it what you may, it is the Mother of all aces waiting to be used if only called out with complete selfless humility and childlike faith. The One is compassion personified waiting to use that ace in the pack. All we need to do is call out with earnestness. You rascal! I know you aren't sleeping. Rudra, don't pretend to snore, wake up, punish me with your ghastly chai.'

Ego is not about personality or individuality but about the refusal to see the inherent truth about oneself.

RUDRA WAS BACK on the mountain with the cross. He had a long climb ahead of him. It was cold on the mountain however nothing mattered to him but to keep climbing and continue cleansing himself. The word Reham kept chanting itself within him. He sought mercy not only for himself but for all those who were on the climb, for all those above him and all those who were struggling below. Every single wrong he had ever done kept flashing through his mind and piercing his heart and he repented and continued the walk. The cross was heavy but far lighter than when he had begun. The higher he climbed the more treacherous the terrain became. He was breathless. He halted and kept the cross by his side. Had he been forgiving of other's mistakes and wrongdoings towards him? He wondered. Not always, he realized, especially when he came from the false pride of righteousness. He had forgiven often but it was an outwardly show, never truly letting go internally. Very often it was just words mouthed not a sense of truly forgiving. He had thus not truly operated from forgiveness and mercy but rather just an attitude of mercy without truly meaning it. He had been fooling himself and others, he realized. It was shameful how often he thought he had truly forgiven but never in reality had lived in the state of forgiveness and mercy. Now he expected all of creation to have mercy on him and mean it. He wanted all of whom he had hurt to forgive him and feel it. He wondered as to why the cosmos should treat him with a light hand when he had not treated anybody with a kind, giving heart? He repented. He wept. He sought forgiveness and mercy and kept chanting Reham. The first thing that erupted from his heart was true forgiveness to all those who had ever hurt him consciously or unknowingly, whether in this lifetime or another. He sent out a prayer forgiving all those who had ever hurt him and sought to release all those from the Karmic bond of hurt, revenge and justice. He truly meant every word that he prayed and he wanted instantly to release all those who had hurt him ever from this Karmic bond. All those who he remembered who had ever hurt him, he prayed for their forgiveness and sought mercy for them and he meant every word, felt every emotion, yearned for every release and in this release he felt liberated, invigorated and reborn. It was as though he had a bath in the most healing spring water and he now felt fresh and rejuvenated. By forgiving and coming from mercy he had done himself the greatest of favours. He had not only released others from the Karmic bond of anger, hate and revenge but he had freed himself too from all the torment and resentment. By forgiving and coming from mercy he had released himself from the crown of thorns that he had forced to adorn himself with.

Then Rudra sought forgiveness and mercy from all those who he had ever hurt and caused pain, in this lifetime and in any lifetime. He pleaded for mercy and

forgiveness and he truly meant every word, felt every pain
and every tear. He prayed to the higher self of all those
whom he had hurt and sought forgiveness and mercy and
slowly, very slowly, he further felt his burden reduce. He
picked up the cross which was far lighter than when he
had rested it and continued his walk up the mountain.

*By forgiving and coming from mercy he had released
himself from the crown of thorns that he had forced
to adorn himself with.*

'BABA, THERE ARE so many paths to spirituality. Which according to You is the most profound?' They were on the beach. It was two thirty in the morning. The brood lay near them exhausted after their play in the water. It was a no moon night. Countless stars lighted the sky and the sea with shimmering rays. The wind blew and it was cold. Baba and Rudra were seated on the soft sand on the beach. The fragrance of the sea was intoxicating. There was not a soul in sight. It was as though in all of creation, only they existed.

'Beta, every path is the right path as long as you avoid the pitfalls of that path. Let me explain to you in a manner that it enters your thick head. Son, there are many who follow the path of destiny and live by the laws of Karma. For them all of creation and all that transpires can be bottled into the laws of cause and effect. They believe that nothing but Karma rules and mankind can do whatever it wants but only the laws of Karma are going to reign eventually. Thus, they do not have much faith in either energy work and charity, not even in prayers, as they are certain that nothing can change one's destiny. They are certain that each one has his or her Karmic blueprint to experience, their cross to carry, mountains to climb, tears to shed and one can only go about it calmly and wisely and be done with this backlog and try not to create new Karma. This is their philosophy. According to them spirituality means going through Karma akin to a woman going through the pangs of childbirth, the pain is excruciating yet joyous as it is all going to be worth it with the birth of the child, or all is going to be worth it through Karmic cleansing.'

'Now, beta, there is nothing wrong with this philosophy but there is a danger of becoming fatalistic or even heartless to the problems of others, as you believe that all is destined, so just bear it with a smile and you want others to walk the same path. Very often the individual does not exert his or her free will to the optimum as the sword of the laws of cause and effect numb the individual. There are countless individuals who worship the laws of Karma to the extent that they become so fatalistic that they become pawns to their limited vision. In India there are countless individuals who truly believe that whatever has to happen shall happen so there is no sense exerting oneself beyond a point. Thus, it is important to respect the laws of Karma but you have to understand that one has to give one's best to each moment and then calmly leave the rest to either Karma or one's lot or one's Goddess, God and Guru. Respect Karma but don't be led by fatalism. Also, don't become heartless or dictated by sheer Karmic logic that you don't help those in need or who reach out to you. So what if you can't go beyond Karma? At least you can give a helping hand to those who are in need and to those who may just need a comforting embrace or even just a kind word.'

'Then, my puppy, there are those who believe in the power of prayers and chanting. For them, spirituality means time spent in prayer. They believe that the more they pray, the more they shall get closer to their Goddess, God and Guru. They may or may not believe in the various other spiritual pathways like, Karma, charity, healing, energy work and meditation, but for them, prayers and more prayers is the way to embrace The One and to protect themselves and their lot from any untoward occurrences. According to them, no matter what you do, eventually your salvation shall come about via prayers and chanting. The danger on this path is that very often the essence of prayers is lost and one becomes a slave to the act. The act of prayer becomes more important than the prayer itself. The number of chants or prayers said or hours spent in prayer overshadow the essence of why one is praying and what true prayer is all about. Prayer is about becoming one with The One. Prayer is about gratitude, seeking forgiveness, mercy. It needs to make you a better human being. But very often the act of prayer overshadows these sublime emotions and makes one a slave to the rituals. It makes one intolerant while praying. It makes many feel more superior due to their act of prayers.'

'Another thing which is very important is that prayers might soften the blow but very often what has been destined shall come to pass. The danger of disillusionment is very great here. I have seen countless good people discontinue their prayers because they believe that their prayers have gone unanswered or they believe that their prayers have not been able to stop the workings of the laws of cause and effect. They have made the mistake of marrying their faith with their prayers. Their faith could be simply a barter arrangement with The One, and I have told you countless times, God is a horrible businessman. Don't ever try and do business with God. Approach The One like a child, not as a business associate. Many pray hoping that their prayers shall be answered. Many pray being certain that their prayers shall be answered. Many have faith that their Goddess, God and Guru shall never disappoint them. Some are certain that The One shall always honour their wishes and what they seek. Beta, but you know better. Things don't work like this. There is something charted out and if you have to go through the experience, you shall go through that experience. No amount of prayers can prevent death from taking place. Eventually death shall knock at every door. There shall be pain, discomfort, disillusionment and hardships, sometimes at an unimaginable scale. If you have been praying for life to be only smooth then you are waiting to be disappointed. If you have been praying to thank The One, seek His and Her mercy, forgiveness and love, then you shall never be disappointed. If your faith is like a business arrangement then no amount of praying is going to help you here.

If your prayers come from gratitude and true love you shall see grace and true love. Why you are praying is going to decide everything eventually. Why are you praying, beta? Are you praying to become one with The One? Ahhhh! *Subhan Allah*, praise be to God! If you are

praying to be enveloped by the energy of The One, praise
be to God. If you are praying to be filled with strength,
calmness, wisdom and grace to go through one's lot with
joyous surrender, God is Great. Why are you praying,
beta, is a question which each person needs to inquire of
himself or herself. Why am I praying? Don't pray to work
out some deal with The One. Please don't. Seek mercy.
Seek forgiveness. Seek protection. Seek blessings. Thank
and thank and thank The One. Seek whatever The One
thinks is best for you and your lot. Don't try and make
deals with the Goddess, God and Guru. Yes, you can put
forward proposals. You can put your proposition before
The One but with one condition, leave everything else
to The One then. You can propose that if your daughter
gets married you shall pay for the marriage of ten poor
girls. Good enough. You seek something personally and
you want to help those in need. Why not? But after you
put forward this proposal go and give your best to get
your daughter married and then have faith that your
Goddess, God and Guru know what is best for your
daughter. Thus, pray for the right reasons and leave the
rest to The One.'

'Then we have those who believe in charity and
some may not believe in charity but believe that in
giving of themselves to serve those in need and the less
privileged is the best way to please one's Lord. Both are
beautifully graceful acts on the spiritual path. But I have
seen tremendous amount of ego enter these good people.
The dangers on this path of spirituality are great. You are
helping people, either personally or through your means,

it is divine. But don't start looking down on those who do not follow this way of yours. There are countless ways to reach The One. You are following one way. Do not look down on those not following your way but walking their individual pathways. Sometimes, those who personally serve, look down on those who indulge in giving charity but not serve those in need in person. Sometimes, those who indulge in charity look down on those who don't follow this way of helping others. The moment you look down on somebody you are moving away from your spiritual objective and your spiritual pathway. Also, no amount of charity shall prevent you from going through things that are meant for you to be experienced. Don't get disillusioned then. Don't make a business arrangement of the largeness of your heart.'

'Then there are those who indulge in fasting or penance or austerity of different kinds to please their Goddess, God and Guru. They sleep less, eat less and speak less. Their way is of meditation. They study the scriptures and can mouth it beautifully. Very often they too get carried away and forget the essence, and the fragrance of humility disappears from them. Imagine, every Tuesday you have resolved not to get angry. Imagine, forty days of fasting of the self off all ego, anger, slander, jealousy, envy, pride and negative thoughts. Wouldn't that be just beautiful and divine? Imagine fasting of all of one's inherent weaknesses every Tuesday or Thursday. Wouldn't that help you much more and also help all of creation much more? And more divine would be if on that day you were to feed three meals

to the poor. Beautiful . . . and so needed. Spread Their
fragrance whenever you can, wherever you can, however
you can and to whomever you can, My child, but don't
judge others who are not walking the same path as you
are. Don't look down on others as then in the name of
spirituality you are indulging in something that is not at
all spiritual.'

'I truly believe each one of these paths of spirituality
are unique in their singularity and individuality but
one needs to embrace every aspect, each pathway, not
looking down upon any, but in fact be certain that there
is a unifying thread which passes through every road, all
eventually leading to that One Door. It is important that
spirituality should not be contained to the individual
but like the musk fragrance, should be spread to one
and all. Even the yogi, who meditates in the Himalayas,
is serving all of mankind, provided he or she intends
to spread the fragrance of his or her meditation for the
well-being of all mankind. In meditation if the yogi
spreads the vibrations of peace and well-being for all
of creation, the yogi, though in some isolated cave,
far away from civilization, is still very much a part
of the fabric of all creation, as the vibrations emitted
sends forth first ripples and then waves upon waves of
well-being, peace, tranquillity and harmony for all of
creation. If the yogi were only concerned about his or
her own salvation, then it would become a self-centred
exercise and the yogi's journey for salvation would
be slow, arduous, and who knows, it might even take
lifetimes. But the moment the yogi seeks not just his or

her salvation but the salvation of all beings, the well-being of all of creation, then the cosmos smiles and helps the spiritual aspirant with momentum which has never been experienced before to achieve not only his or her own goal but also to assist all of creation.'

'All the Masters put the well-being of all of creation before Their personal interest. The very fact that the Masters do not take the final leap into The Great Fire that allows Them to merge with The One and thus, become The One, is because They love Their children so much, that They want to help each and every one to first merge and only then consider Their work to be complete. My brother, the Great Taj, Tajuddin Baba, was very clear when He said that till He did not help in making one lakh and twenty thousand (1,20,000) Saints on earth, He would not rest or take the final leap towards liberation of His own self by merging with The One. This is what spirituality is about. Spreading the fragrance of The One to all and not trying to use it for one's own individual ego, power or advancement. It is meant for everybody's well-being. Every time an individual grows truly spiritual, it helps all of creation, beta. But the important thing is to grow truly spiritual which is never an individualistic back alley but a highway through which countless travellers pass through. You have to become that highway, you gnome, not some secret tunnel; this is most important. I fear nowadays personal growth has become more important than universal well-being. Everybody is more concerned about his or her own personal growth than spreading the fragrance to one and all. There is nothing spiritual about this. Share your fragrance and see how beautifully you shall grow too. Share yourself to become whole. All spirituality has to be holistic and never individualistic. If we meditate or pray only for oneself or one's near and dear ones and not for one and all, it means we adhere to the philosophy of diversity and not of true Oneness. If Oneness does not exist then true spirituality does not exist. If our prayers do not involve those who are not in our orbit, the unfortunate, the dying, the starving, the meek, the damned, the bullied, the tortured, the ailing, the lonely, the defeated, those left behind, the earth bound or those who have gone astray, we are not truly walking the path of spirituality. We are in a car that is truly not moving anywhere but is in fact stationary, in the illusion of it moving ahead. If each moment is not spent in spreading the Light and Compassion of The One, then, there is something we are doing wrong. Just prayers, just charity, just visions, just prophecy—is never enough, it remains . . . just something, not everything. It is not inclusive, but exclusive, and there is no place for exclusivity but always room for inclusiveness. It has to be a composition, a symphony of all the right notes creating the right music with all the right instruments. If we do not use every bit of ourselves with every bit of all that we have got, then the scenery keeps changing due to the illusionary projector behind us but we are rooted at the same spot, like those photography studios of earlier days, where cut-outs of monuments and travel destinations kept changing behind you while you sat rooted to one spot, in some cut-out vehicle, a car or a plane; you were seated on the same seat while the backdrop kept changing behind you; all shadow-boxing, nobody went anywhere.'

'Whether you communicate with your Goddess, God and Guru or every known and unknown spirit in Creation; whether you pray all day or heal or provide financial help, always remember the essence of spirituality is to enrich each moment, not just yours but all those whom we are associated with, directly or indirectly, and it needs to be embraced in its totality. Like a meal, that needs various ingredients, some in minuscule quantum, so minuscule that you might not think it really makes any difference whether it is part of the dish or not, but a true chef knows that every ingredient helps in creating that Master Dish, similarly, spirituality is all about embracing and unifying and being all inclusive. The Sun would lose some part of its radiance if one of the seven rays was missing from it.'

'I understand that all of us cannot do everything. There are some who truly can't contribute financially as they themselves are trying their level best to keep body and soul together. But they can give of their goodness, their kindness, their smile, just by being decent individuals, selflessly praying for all in creation, spreading love and laughter and tenderness and sheer goodness. Their contribution or charity or projection of compassion, may not be in cash or kind, or even their time, but of their very essence and that divine spark that lurks in each one of us, very often so deep within us that it might as well not exist, but it does exist. A short prayer for those going through pain and discomfort of various intensities does not take too much time. Spirituality in all its totality is the only way to go forward on this beautiful though infuriating journey. Be the best of who you can be, beta. Do the best of what you can do. Live the best of how you can live. Give the best of what you can give. By just striving to give each moment your absolute best, trust me, you will reach your destination.'

'But, Baba, this road is not that simple. First of all to be able to connect and live in the moment or connect with The One doesn't happen so often. Why? I mean, I get all that You told me but why is it that the connect with one's Goddess, God and Guru doesn't take place every time I sit for prayer, chanting or meditation. Sometimes it takes place but most often it doesn't. Why is that? Why is it that even when I can connect sometimes, that connection doesn't last all day but for a short period of time? It's there but then slowly fades away?'

'Oh my sweet nincompoop child, always remember that we are not the body. No matter how insignificant our lives or our own self-worth may seem to be, the fact is that, within us there is life, and life emanates from The Creator, and thus within us resides The One, and thus, each one of us is truly significant. We are the energy that resides within the body. We are the spark from that Great Flame, a drop from that Great Ocean, a tune from that Great Orchestra, a sigh from the Great Breath. We are not what we seem to be. Just like we are aware that the Sun does not rise or set, but still we go about believing it does. We know that darkness doesn't come about because the Sun has set but only because a part of the earth has shown its back to the sun, hence the ensuing darkness. We all know this but we all seem to forget this each day. So much so that in a regular conversation one says that the sun is setting and the sun is rising, in spite of knowing the reality that the sun doesn't rise or set. Beta, within us resides the Spark of divinity, Shakti that keeps the body and soul together. Without this Shakti, the body would drop dead. We are a part of that Energy, in the form of consciousness, individual consciousness; some would call it consciousness, some would call it the mind, some would call it individuality, some would call it the soul, some the atma, but the fact is that our body is not us and we are not the body, we are this Energy, consciousness, individuality, soul, atma, in the body. When our bodies die, we do not cease to exist. When our bodies change or there is some amputation, we do not cease to exist, we are who we are, not because of the body, but because of our individual consciousness.'

'Within us resides all that resides in the Paramatma, The Prime Soul, The Creator, the Goddess, God, Primordial Guru. We are the spark from that Great Flame. Whatever the Great Flame contains, the spark shall contain too. The One resides in each one of us. You need to dive within to reach that Pearl. Now, pertaining to your question, if an individual was to sit silently and pray, meditate or chant, without the certain belief and realization that he or she is not the body, then what takes place is we have already begun with duality rather than Oneness. If I am not coming from energy consciousness but from body consciousness, then I come forth from duality as the body stands between you and The One. You believe you are the body, which means you are separate from The One. So, first and foremost, if you believe that you are not the body but the energy in the body, when you sit to pray, chant, meditate, you begin with the complete realization that you are the energy, connecting to the Prime Energy, your Mother Source, your source of origin. When you begin your prayer or meditation, with the complete understanding that you too are energy and you are connecting with your Source, your Origin, which is one and the same thing, that you are the spark from the Great Flame, drop from the Great Ocean, you begin with Oneness. You begin with an existing connect and a real foundation to build on. When you do not commence with this simple philosophy then you commence with duality; you are the body, you are separate, and you want to connect with the Great Flame, which is the Great Energy, which is something completely different from who you are, and the worst possible thing for you to believe is that this Great Energy is not inside you, but is something external, which now you have to bring forth within you and then you need to become one with It. All this happens because you are coming forth from an external source; identifying yourself as somebody else and the great Energy as somebody else. You are yourself and this great Energy is far away, some alien entity that you now need to befriend and make One with yourself. Please, for God's sake, tell Me you understand this, beta, as I am worried, seeing that completely blank look on your face that you don't get a word that I am saying.'

'My Lord and Master, I understand every word that comes out of Your holy and pious mouth.'

'*Badmash!* Okay. So the first thing each individual on the path of spirituality has to understand, has to make clear, has to be a hundred per cent certain of, is that "I am not the body, I am the spark from the Great Flame, I am part of the universal Shakti that flows through all of creation." Till this is not clear and not certain, it is very difficult to achieve the state of Oneness that you are talking about, each time you sit to pray, chant and meditate. It just won't happen as you shall come from duality, seeking Oneness, rather than come from Oneness to perpetuate the state of unison.'

'So, let us take for example that an individual sits for meditation attached to the illusionary state of him or her being separate from The One. Now even if the person were to try and go within, focus on breathing, begin to meditate or pray or chant The Name, till the sense of duality persists, Oneness will not take place because your attention will always be external since your search is external. I am searching for The One to enter me or I have the picture of my Goddess, God and Guru in mind, thus, though my eyes are shut, am breathing, chanting, praying or meditating, my true being is outside myself, external, either with my Guru's face or statue in mind or waiting for the Energy to flow within me. So, in reality, I am not within but am actually outside. I am waiting for the Energy to fill me up. I am hoping for some sign. I am imagining that I am with my Master or His or Her Energy is entering me, but all this while in reality, I am outside, external. Then slowly I begin to feel the Energy within me and surging within me and I experience various things, see various things and then I have to get up. For how long can these sensations abide within me as subconsciously I believe that I have, through prayers, chanting, and meditation, got these sensations or Energy within me, but as I get out of this state, life slowly takes over and I believe these sensations and Energy have again left me, till the next time I sit for meditation again.'

'How do I allow these sensations and this Energy to always be present within me? The answer is really simple. When I believe that I am not the body but the spark of the Great Flame, and the Great Flame through this spark always resides within me. Then I begin my prayers, chanting, and meditation, already aware that the Great Flame resides within me. Just as I am aware when I am eating, bathing, working, talking, going about life, knowing that this Great Flame resides within me, through the spark within me, I already am in Oneness even before I sit for meditation. I am not trying to be in Oneness, I *am* Oneness, as I am not this body, but the energy in this body and this energy is the spark of the Great Flame. When I chant The Name, I am not calling out to the One, outside me, that please come to me or enter me or be within me. No, I am doing the very opposite. I already know that The One is within me; I am just trying to make the Fire grow stronger within me. I am trying to wake up The One within me or make The One within me further awakened. I am already internal. I am only going further within. **I am only trying to clean the**

mirror so that I can see my true self more clearly. I am trying to fan the flame and make it into a raging fire within me. So, every time I chant The Name or pray or meditate, I do it with the surety that the Energy already resides within me and my duty and dharma, my sole and soul purpose of life is to bring forth His and Her Presence with greater intensity awakened within me. If it is dormant then to wake up the Energy, if it is a slight flame then to fan that flame into a fire, if it is a fire then become one with that Fire, but all is within me, as I am the spark of that Great Flame. There is nothing external, it is all internal within me; it is Me. There is no difference between the spark and the Great Flame, it is all One. By believing this and then praying, chanting, meditating, working, bathing, speaking, doing anything, one only goes more and more within. The One who is dormant in our spiritual genes, gets woken up, and then begins to operate from our very within. The more you wake up the Energy within, the more She or He operates from our very within. We need to believe that The One resides within us and through our prayers, chants, breath, the flame becomes a Fire. We have to slowly fan the flame. We need to slowly and tenderly wake up our Goddess, God and Guru who resides within us. The more we pray or meditate or live this way, being certain that She or He resides within, sleeping like a child, tenderly, like a mother wakes up the child, if we keep at it, one day, we will feel The One within awakened and that will be the first step towards self-realization and also become one with all the mystical treasures which one has within our own selves. From within we need to dive in further. Never external to internal, beta, as everything is already within. Then when we come out of our prayers, chants and meditation, we shall continue to feel The One within us and who knows, maybe even for the entire day, as you and The One are not two separate entities but are One. Thus, knowing that you are a part of The One, slowly you too shall become The One. But this needs to come from within and to go further within. Not you to come from duality and seek Oneness. Search for The One within you, and by operating from being the energy within you, you will activate the dormant memory of you and the Goddess as The One. This is how you will then live through the day and be in Oneness. Whenever you feel the duality, you go back into prayer, meditate and reconnect with the Great Fire. The more you do so constantly, the more you will live in this state of Oneness. If you and I are created by The One, then we imbibe The One within us. It may be in a very dormant state or not in a state of dynamic magnitude, but each one of us has to have within us all that the Creator embodies or the same Divine Presence. You have to believe in this reality. The Great Fire that burns within each of us has the power to light up the cosmos, don't roam about in circles in the dark. The truth of life is that in each being exists The One.'

Baba then stood up and they all walked back to the cottage. It was nearing five. Rudra put the water to boil and the coal to heat. By the time he slept, it was dawn. Baba sat on His rug and was deep in meditation. The brood slept in the veranda and life was good, life was cool.

We are the energy that resides within the body. We are the spark from that Great Flame, a drop from that Great Ocean, a tune from that Great Orchestra, a sigh from the Great Breath. We are not what we seem to be.

RUDRA WAS BACK on the mountain with Baba in the village. He could see, in real life, what Baba had explained the previous night. He could see the difference, of those who operated with the knowledge that they were not the body but the energy within, the spark from The Great Flame, and those who for some reason thought everything was external and they and The One were separate entities. The difference between these two groups was clear. Those who believed that they were a part of The Great Flame, went about their day in Oneness. They were not seeking Oneness, they knew that they were a part of the Oneness. Their thoughts, words, deeds came forth from this realization. Whether they sat to pray, chant, meditate, work, bathe and eat, they did so coming from Oneness not only within themselves but with everybody around them. It showed in their demeanour. They came from a certain space of peace and contentment no matter what they indulged in. It showed in their vibrations. There was a certain stillness about them. This was not apparent in those who came from duality. Those who thought The One existed outside them were peaceful till they prayed, chanted and meditated but soon after they re-entered the world, their vibrations changed from stillness to restlessness. They came from duality and it showed

in their conduct with each moment. It was palpable.
It didn't matter how spiritual they were, they lost the
fragrance after a while. Rudra realized how complicated
we have made our lives. We have forgotten who we
truly are, what is contained within us and what throbs
within us. The Shakti that is clearly flowing through us
we denied Her existence through our duality and then
searched for Her outside us. Like the musk deer, we went
in search of the fragrance that, in reality, was within us.

Those who believed that they were a part of The Great Flame,
went about their day in Oneness. They were not seeking
Oneness that they knew they were a part of the Oneness.

RUDRA SPENT THE next few days channelling while Baba was not physically present. He did all the housework and made sure the oil lamps were constantly lit. He spent his days taking care of the brood and also drove about in his van replenishing stock for survival. On the third day when he parked the van he knew Baba was back. He and the brood rushed into the cottage and found Baba seated in meditation but with a broad smile on His face. He then opened an eye and chuckled as they all rushed to Him like children to a parent who has returned home after a long time. The day passed beautifully. It was night. They had their chai, biscuits and smoked a chillum and then went for a stroll to the beach. It was only ten but there was nobody on the beach as usual. The first smile of the new moon adorned the clear sky and they walked for a while in silence. Then Baba sat down and Rudra seated himself in front of Him. Blondie sat with them while Boy and Girl ran about in the water.

'Baba, teach me how to pray. I know I need to come from Oneness but there are many who might not be able to do so and I am sure that there are various ways to pray and if one does pray from the heart all prayers are heard.'

'Yes, my manic child. It is true. So listen carefully. First how not to pray, beta, as often the calling becomes a mere ritual. The pitfalls are so subtle and yet create great stagnation or worse even make the seeker lose his or her way without even realizing it. So take a simple but noble act of chanting and saying one's prayers. Initially, we all begin with the right intention, commitment, focus, dedication and love. But as time passes by, our chanting and our prayers become more of a routine, a box to be ticked, mundane. Thus, what began as a noble calling has got reduced to a formality, a duty. Thus, though we are chanting and praying, the essence is no longer present, the Oneness is absent and unfortunately we are oblivious of indulging in just a self-gratifying, ego-boosting ritual. When there is no heart, focus, plea, yearning, love, gratitude in our prayers, the voice, and the energy, our call, doesn't reach Home, but gets lost in the by-lanes of one's daily schedule.'

'Yet we think that we are praying, chanting, creating shields of protection and walking the path of *sadhna*, the religious traditions or Oneness. We could be spending hours in a day, in a so called prayer or spiritual pursuits and even feel truly gratified and ecstatic about sticking to our schedule but unfortunately the most noble of all callings has been reduced to just that, a schedule, a time table, a box to be ticked; no longer a commune with the Goddess, God and Guru, either externally or within.'

'When we assume that we are in prayer or even in meditation and feel truly gratified about our own dedication, love and discipline, often, in reality, most of us are only caught up with completing our to-do list, like brushing teeth in the morning, having a bath, eating meals, going about doing the day's work. **The spiritual pursuits have no fragrance of love, humility or yearning and we are not even aware of it**. This could go on for years and decades and we are under the illusion of walking the Path of prayers.

'When our entire being is not in prayer, we have somehow made the most sublime part of our existence into a force of habit which needs completion. There is no prayer taking place, just muttering of ancient words. No chanting happening, just chatter of well-constructed words being indulged in. No true commune with The One, in fact, no commune with oneself too. I have told you this often, beta.'

'Yes, Baba.'

'When one's twenty-four hours are spent in those hours or even minutes which one spends in prayer or any other type of spiritual pursuit, now we have woven the time for prayer as one of the things to be done and dusted, each day. Spiritual pursuit is not an act, it is one's very reason for existence. Something one does not just do but lives for and eventually becomes. It is not something to be over with, but it is a state we should want to be in every waking moment of our lives. So, my frog, before you begin to pray, each day meditate on how not to pray and then begin to pray. This is most important. On how to live sometimes one needs to remember one's death and mortality each day, similarly how to pray comes forth from remembering how not to pray each day. Do that always, every day, for the rest of eternity, every time before you begin to say your prayers. Will you, my defrosted fossil?'

Rudra nodded. He knew how important these words were as he knew how each day he forgot how not to pray, resulting in not praying with the intensity, yearning, love and devotion that were mandatory.'

'Also, beta, understand that if you have the opportunity to sit and pray then you have been blessed with the privilege of being allowed to sit in commune with The One. **It is an honour and a privilege to be able to pray and one needs to be blessed with the Karma or the destiny to be able to do that**. Everybody does not have the privilege to spend time in prayer, beta. Their lives and circumstances might not grant them this opportunity to pray. We have worked lifetimes to be able to come to this place in our existence where we can sit and pray and pursue spirituality and spiritual practices. We have worked lifetimes to cultivate the inclination to pray and this opportunity should not be wasted. This opening to be able to have the inclination to pray and the need to pray should not be taken lightly and this opportunity should not be wasted away. Why is it that some of us have the inclination, time, place, energy, to be able to walk the Path of prayers and so many don't? Why is it that, all of a sudden, the need to pray has arisen after years? Why is it that after praying for years or decades suddenly the inclination or the opportunity to continue with one's spiritual practices dries out? Even to be able to get the environment, time or inclination to spend time in prayer is because in some lifetime we have worked towards this. We have created a destiny that has allowed us to make this Path our priority or a way of life in this lifetime and now we are partaking of the fruit of our intent and hard work from some other lifetime. But remember, the sand is flowing. We have accumulated a quantum of Karma to be able to pray too and either we keep refilling that sand glass or we let the sand fritter away. Nothing is permanent. Everything has been accounted for and there is a time period for everything. Either we increase our lot or let it waste away as a formality. We have been blessed with a certain number of hours to be able to become one with The One. Let us say that an individual has earned the Karma to pray. He or she has got the opportunity of a thousand hours of prayers or any other spiritual pursuit. Now the question is would we like to use each minute of each hour of those thousand hours in dedicated pursuit, thereby increasing the number of hours through our dedication and earnestness or do we squander away those thousand hours and then be left with nothing? Would we like to waste those precious hours gifted to us by Providence and our own hard work of some lifetime and convert grace into a formality and a box to be ticked off as a routine, or would we like to make the most of this opportunity and make each second in each minute in each hour count, and in fact, increase the end total through our complete Oneness to prayers? From every grain that enters our mouth to every opportunity for prayer, there is a count, a meter ticking away, sand flowing through. There are no free meals in the cosmos. We have earned the right for every blessing and every good fortune that we enjoy and we are responsible for every baggage and cross that we carry and everything comes with an expiry date. Do we want to squander grace and convert it into a formality or do we want to take this opportunity and convert it into everlasting grace, is in our hands. Common sense says that when you have dedicated a certain amount of time for prayer, it is best to give one's best to that certain time, and live in that moment. Why squander away the time and the opportunity? Anyway, you are going to sit for that amount of time for prayer. Give it your best and immerse yourself into your devotion. Why waste the opportunity? When we pray we should be convinced that our prayers have such purity that whoever we are praying to is truly hearing our prayer. When we sit to pray, the fragrance of our prayers should force our Goddess, God and Guru to keep everything aside and listen to our call, be filled with our *pukar,* be one with our prayer too. **When you pray with such intensity that The One shall listen to your prayer, then your purity, intensity, devotion and yearning will get wings to reach The One**. The certainty that our prayers shall reach whoever we pray to, if done with complete devotion and love, will fuel our prayers and make sure our prayers reach our Loved One.'

'Baba, how does one do this? We don't even know where The One resides?'

'You constipated gnat, there are three ways you can do this. You can either pray as though our Goddess, God and Guru is in the Spirit Dimension where They reside and we are reaching out to Them. We hope Our prayer reaches Them wherever They reside. The greater the intensity, love and yearning to be heard, shall open pathways for our prayers to reach Them. This is called the external prayer. It is a call to Them.

'Then there is the internal prayer I taught you the other day about how we are certain that They reside within us and thus our attention is directed within. We can pray to Them, assured that They are hearing us because They reside within us, either in a dormant state or some state of wakefulness. Usually, for most people it is in the state of dormancy, so we need to wake Them up. The only way to awaken Them so they can operate through us from within is by making our prayers so intense that They have no option but to wake up and begin to operate through us. Our prayers need to have that purity, intensity and fragrance to awaken Them. They then begin to throb in each cell of ours and fill our very breath, vibrations and being.'

'Then there is the third way of reaching out to Them. This is when we are certain that They reside not only in Their celestial abode, wherever that place may be, but also within us, within each being. This prayer needs greater focus as now we believe that They are within as well as outside. They reside in Their heavenly abode as well as within us. They are outside us and also within us. They are everywhere. So now we not only have to pray with the intensity of a mad person trying to make our voice heard, but also to awaken Them within us. So, the force has to have enough fuel to reach the external dimension and have the power to awaken Them from Their dormant state within.'

'When was the last time you prayed with this kind of intensity and *junoon*, beta, will decide the last time you really prayed. Imagine, They want to hear your prayer, want to see that intensity but all that They hear and witness is mouthing of words, while your mind is far away. Imagine, They are present in front of you, hoping to be enveloped with the purity and fragrance of your prayer but instead hear some rattling of words, with no depth, no love and no focus, just a ramble, a routine that must be done with. Wouldn't that be a sad moment for you, my child?'

'They have given us twenty-four hours with each hour consisting of sixty minutes and each minute throbbing with sixty seconds. Countless seconds make a day. How many seconds do we really remember Them with true love and intensity out of those? When we instill awareness and gratitude into our prayers, when we pray with earnest yearning and seek mercy, when we call out to Them like a child who is seeking one's very Mother. **When our prayers are not a ritual or a formality but our very reason for existence, then we have begun to walk the true Path of prayers**. Every time we take Their Name and we are aware of it, our awareness makes our prayer reach Them. Thus, it would be a shame to waste this opportunity that we have of spending time in prayer and spiritual pursuits, as this opportunity does not come to all and doesn't come without working for it and there is an expiry date if we don't allow more grace to enter. This is our gift and if we squander this honour away, then who knows when and in which lifetime we might earn the privilege to be able to get an opportunity to pray as and when we would so desire. Pray as though you are possessed of the Divine Spirit; pray like a child yearning for the embrace of a loved one; pray as though it may be the last time you might get the opportunity to pray. Pray that They have taken time off and are hearing us pray. Do not disregard Them by making your prayers a formality. Then you have debased the only truly noble thing a human being can indulge in, which involves Them directly with yourself, and nothing in between. This is the eternal truth, beta.'

Baba stood up and they walked back to the cottage. Rudra had prepared a simple curry for Baba and he had cut apples and made a homemade *paan*. Baba ate a little bit of everything as then they sat down with their chai and chillum and saw the night embrace the sea. After a while they could only hear the waves sing their soft lullaby.

Spiritual pursuit is not an act, it is one's very reason for existence. Something one does not just do but lives for and eventually becomes.

BABA HALTED AT a village on the mountain with Rudra. The villagers were all involved in prayer of some kind. Rudra could see clearly how one's intensity while in prayer made all the difference to those who prayed. It was all about one's intent and devotion. Those who were one in prayer, their vibrations glowed in various intensities and were luminous, while those who prayed as a formality, there was absolutely no change in their aura and vibrations. Greater the intensity, more luminous were the auras and vice versa. Rudra could see various energies enter those who were deep in prayer and various cleansing and healing taking place. Rudra could see the aura glow brighter. He could see various Spirit bodies come forth to bless and heal those who prayed with love and devotion while those who prayed as a formality, there was absolutely no change in either the auras or luminousness as well as no energies working on them. It wasn't about what they prayed for or how they prayed but it was all about the intensity and devotion with which the prayers were said; loudly or internal, it did not make that much of a difference. It was all about what kind of love and devotion the prayers were chanted with. It did not matter what they were doing while praying, it was all about where their mind and intent were during prayers.

Some sat still and prayed but Rudra could make out their minds were elsewhere as there was absolutely no impact on their auras and vibrations. While some went about their jobs, internally praying and chanting, and Rudra could see their auras being healed and worked upon. Some prayed to their Masters who themselves had not reached a level of Oneness and though they prayed with intensity the level of work on their auras was limited. Rudra understood that if you seek something from a source, the source too should be brimming with what you seek. If you prayed to somebody, who was still a work-in-progress, then you received only what could be sourced; nothing more, nothing less.

He sat near an old man who prayed to a Guru who on Mother Earth at this very moment was very popular. Yes, energy work was taking place but the intensity was far less than those who prayed to Those who were already in the ocean of Oneness. Thus, Rudra realized how important it was to pray to the right source too. Those who prayed to the Creator in the formless state benefitted the most as they prayed to the Original form of Energy, Shakti, who always was, is and will be, without any corruption and without any hindrances. Those who prayed to the Creator, Shakti, as sheer Energy, no form, just pure Energy, derived the greatest amount of Light and Energy and their auras shone the brightest. The Name did not matter to the Primordial One. Goddess, Ahura, Allah, God, Creator, The Supreme One, all prayers reached the Primordial Energy, The Goddess Creator. Without form, who always was, is and shall be. But eventually it was with what intensity you prayed that gave you the greatest of all healing and benefit.

Rudra could see countless spirit guides working on those who prayed with the right devotion and love. The spirit guides worked on the devotees in such a sublime manner that one needed to see it to understand the love they had for each individual absorbed in prayer. The more Oneness in prayer the greater that force surrounded them. It was as though the spirit guides had no option but to come forth and surround the one in prayer and heal and cleanse. Rudra looked at Baba and Baba smiled tenderly—then Rudra could not see Baba but only saw Light and Radiance. He wasn't present in the body. He was a source of Radiance and His Radiance had no beginning and no end. He was merged with the radiance of Oneness. He was present everywhere and there was Radiance amongst those who prayed. Whether they prayed to Him or not, as He was one with the Source, He too was the Source and thus He too was present with all those who prayed to the Oneness Shakti.

Without form, who always was, is and shall be. But eventually it was with what intensity that you prayed that gave you the greatest of all healing and benefit.

BABA WALKED AHEAD and Rudra followed on the beach. Blondie was with them. Boy and Girl had gone out to some place but they would return, like they so often did. Blondie never left Baba and Rudra's side. It was four in the morning. Baba had prayed all through the night and Rudra had been busy with the housework and preparing packets of food for the brood. Once a week he prepared the weekly ration of food for his brood and put it in the cold storage and every day heated the contents of the packet for their lunch and dinner. Rudra then prepared chai and chillum. After Baba and he had finished the tea and smoked the chillum, they went for their walk. There was nobody around. The beach was theirs and it was pitch dark. The sky was filled with clouds and the moon was not to be seen. There were hardly any stars visible in the sky. There was a slight breeze and it was warm. The sea had withdrawn and Baba sat down with Rudra in front of Him. Blondie sat between both the men, facing Baba.

'Baba, tell me more about prayers?'

'My idiot child, when you sit to pray assuming that this is the last time you shall get the opportunity to pray, the intensity of one's prayers will increase to another level. Beta, when one leaves the body is something between The One who controls destiny and who keeps an account of the breaths one has taken. Our lifespan is not determined by the number of years but by the number of breaths. Each being has a particular number of breaths to his or her account. Dogs pass over mostly by the age of fifteen and then there are turtles that live over a hundred years. Dogs are perpetually panting and use their quantum of breath faster. The yogis manipulate their life span by manipulating their breath.'

'Thus, first and foremost, focus on your breath and make the breathing calm. Then you sit for prayers and pray as though it is the last time you shall have the privilege to pray ever again, then the quality of your prayer, the depth of your prayer, the intensity of your prayer, the yearning in your prayers, merged with the calmness of your breath, shall create a powerful vibration of purity and focus, which shall reach The One that we pray to. The call from the very depths of our being, shall be heard for sure, this I assure you, My pickle-headed child.'

'Imagine, if we knew we would never get the opportunity to pray again for whatever reason, how would you pray to your Goddess, God and Guru then? Imagine if we were going to be judged by the last prayer we ever prayed, how would we pray? I am sure we would pray with an intensity that we lack while we normally sit for prayer. Remember, beta, whatever one thinks at the time of death decides where we gravitate to. This is how important each thought is and this is how important one's prayers are. Every time you sit for

prayers imagine this could be your last prayer and this is
the prayer that you shall be gauged with and heard with.
Imagine as though it is your reality. Then sit for prayer
as though this is the last time you shall truly commune
with The One. Imagine it. Believe it. Then sit and
pray. See the difference. See the new-found intensity
that you are filled with. You are never going to be in
commune with The One ever again. This is your last
chance. How are you going to pray then, my child?
You shall pray as though your very life depended on
that prayer. When we sit to pray and we pray as though
we might never get the opportunity for prayer ever
again then the prayer traverses through time and space
and calls out to The One in sheer earnest: 'Hear me for
the last time, my Lord and Master. Please hear me as I
might not be able to pray again, my Goddess. Hear me,
please, and bless me, please.' This is the simplest and the
most effective way to reach out. The intensity will be
immense, trust Me, My worm.'

'The other way to create intensity in our prayers is
to pray as though there is an emergency. You will realize
that if there is an emergency in our lives or there is fear or
a great want, suddenly our prayers become exceedingly
intense and our focus is right and there is a yearning
and plea in our call which is usually absent when we
sit to pray. If we are in trouble, somebody is sick, you
are petrified about something, the intensity in prayers
increases countless number of times more than normal.
During an emergency, the intensity in our prayers is so
strong that it can rarely be matched at normal times.

It is as if our entire lives and all that is sane and peaceful, depend upon your prayers being heard, thus the focus which one's prayer takes on during such times is incomparable. There is a plea, a cry, a yearning, which is never there when everything is fine or as good or as bad as it usually always is. And then when things settle down, the emergency is a distant memory, our prayers become a part of another to-do list, to be done with and gotten over with. When there is nothing extraordinary taking place our prayers too are very ordinary. Thus, the intensity of prayers is directly in proportion to the emergency or lack of emergency at hand. If things are really low then our prayers reach a greater height. Those times our plea to the Oneness Family comes from the depth of our very being and it is as though each cell has become one with the prayer, which is more like a cry for help. And when all is normal, the intensity of our prayers seem to be more of a formality, a mere routine. Thus, pray as though it is the last time you shall get the honour to pray but also pray as though the life of our loved ones depends on our prayers.'

'Also pray with the firm belief that you are being heard. Pray with the firm conviction that our prayers are going to reach our Goddess, God and Guru, and believe that whoever we are praying to, our prayers shall reach Them. Imagine Them hearing you, be it from Their celestial abode, be it within you, be it standing in front of you. Can you imagine if you prayed being assured that your prayers are being heard, how beautifully intense your prayers shall be? Imagine if you were certain that your Goddess, God and Guru were standing in front of you, attentive to all that you prayed for, wouldn't your prayers take on a different intensity? When we are assured that our Goddess, God and Guru, is either hearing us, seated in front of us, within us, or hearing us from Their celestial abode, our prayers shall take on a different intensity.'

'Thus, when we pray, pray with the belief and the purity that whomever we are praying to is hearing our plea. Believe in this. Then see the devotion that flows forth from you. It shall have a divine fragrance. Our prayers may not be answered but just being certain that our prayers are being heard itself shall make all the difference. Whether our prayer shall be answered or granted is a matter of destiny and dependent on the largest good for all concerned, which is a different matter, but at least knowing and being assured from within that our prayers are being heard shall make you pray with an intensity which has never arisen before. Our focus shall completely be with The One and with our prayer. There shall be depth, clarity, yearning, purity and truth in our prayer as we know that The One is hearing us out; She or He is within us, in front of us, hearing us.'

'It is only when we think of prayers as a mandatory formality that our prayers start lacking the purity and concentration. It is like chanting a particular prayer or mantra for a number of times. We usually just rush through the entire process to complete the count. Even your Goddess, God and Guru will be astounded at how fast you have completed your prayer and chant. But if you are certain that you are being heard, if you are certain that The One is awake and hearing your chant, either within you, or in the celestial abode or in front of you; when you truly believe She or He is present, then automatically your prayer and your chant will take on a very different intensity and shall be done properly, calmly, patiently and in complete awareness. It will no longer be a formality but a calling.'

'But, Baba, sometimes one has decided to pray a number of *malas* or rosary and speed is of essence.'

'My silly rabbit, when you know that you are being heard, even if you chant with speed, there will be clarity in your chant and a focus in your prayer. That shall not be compromised. The love in your prayer will be ever present. That is why the other day I told you to pray as though The One resides within oneself, may be in a dormant form, and our entire focus is to awaken The One within. When that shall become your focus to awaken The One within you, trust Me, you will want to be heard and you will be certain about being heard, your prayers will exude a very beautiful intensity and fragrance. Thus, pray as though it is the last time you shall have the privilege of being able to pray. Pray as though your life depends upon it and pray being assured that your prayers are being heard.'

'Now comes the most important aspect of prayer. Pray because you truly love The One you are praying to, thus pray with true love. Imagine if your loved one were to tell you that he or she loves you as a mere

formality. There is no love involved, it's just a duty.
Would you want such kind of affirmation of love? I
don't think so. Imagine your child were to come and
tell you a hundred and eight times a day . . . 'I love you,
I love you, I love you . . .' as a mere duty and formality,
a to-do list. Would you want such an affirmation of such
words? No. You would rather have your loved one tell
you just once a day, 'I truly love you' . . . wouldn't that
be much better? That is why it is not for how long we
pray but with what feeling we pray, beta. Yes, if you
can pray with true feeling for however long we could
pray with love and devotion that would be divine and
sublime. It is not how much we pray but with what
kind of love we pray. It is not how complicated the
prayer is, but how simple and childlike our prayer and
the way we pray is.'

'So, our prayers need to be said with love. We need
to truly love The One. It should come forth from love
and gratitude. Not come forth from words and a sense
of responsibility and formality. Just as we don't want our
loved ones to work out a deal with us or we don't want
our loved ones to treat us as a financial account or be
with us because of what we can give them or how we
can protect them, the same way, we too need to pray
coming forth only from love and gratitude. We want
our loved ones to love us because they truly love us and
respect the fact that sometimes we shall have to refuse
them certain things, even though we can easily afford
giving them what they seek, because we know it is not
for their highest good. Thus, we too need to pray having

faith in Their highest wisdom. We need to pray with pure love, not as a barter system, not for doing business, not as a to-do list.'

'And most importantly, when you pray not seeking anything but Their blessings, Their presence and Their love that prayer is the most sublime of all prayers. When your prayer is not a business deal but just an expression of your love and gratitude, the fragrance of that prayer has no comparison. The prayer that comes from humility and gratitude, seeking forgiveness, wisdom and strength to go through whatever is in store for us with calmness, compassion and complete surrender to Their wisdom and love, is the best prayer, as we are not seeking for our Karma to be manipulated, we are not seeking things, we just want to make Them happy and proud of us. Praying to Them to help us give each moment our very best and to leave the rest to Their wisdom and grace, joyously, is a prayer as good as any prayer found in any scripture here or beyond. Remember, my child, when you pray like this, drop-by-drop the ocean will fill up. Prayers that come from a tranquil heart, a heart filled with gratitude and pure selfless love becomes akin to an oasis for a traveller walking through the desert and the hot sands of the laws of cause and effect. What is the purpose of prayer, beta? To express love and gratitude, to seek forgiveness and mercy, to be able to go through life gracefully and joyously no matter what and to eventually move away from duality and darkness into Oneness and Radiance. When you reach The One you pray to or when you pull The One towards yourself, either you travel to The

One or you pull The One to you or awaken The One within you. There needs to be power for anything to defy gravity or to go within, to the womb of Mother Earth. Our prayers, if not fueled with intense pure love, gratitude and yearning, will not have the power to go through and go beyond the beyond; either move upwards or go deep within. If you pray with the right love and intensity eventually you shall reach the stage where you shall need no external pilgrimages, no paraphernalia, no priest, no flame, no fruits, no flowers, nothing. You are the devotee praying to The One within you. Eventually, you are praying and being prayed to. You are the one chanting and being chanted to, and then duality ceases, all that remains is you and you too are The One. You are The One.'

Baba stood up and stretched. He then looked at Rudra and smiled. Blondie stood up and stretched too. She too looked at Rudra and it seemed as though she smiled too. Rudra raised his eyes and he too stretched. Then he gave a broad smile too. They walked towards the cottage. The clouds had drifted away. The moon smiled back at them. They reached the cottage and Rudra put the water to boil and the coal to heat. He heard Baba humming some ancient Sufi song. He didn't understand a word as it was in Farsi, but he shut his eyes and took a deep breath. A cool breeze caressed Rudra. He stood in front of the gas stove and saw small bubbles erupt in the water and the fragrance of the burning coal. He took a plate and placed various edibles on it. In the background Baba's voice could be heard. It was the most divine voice and Rudra shut his eyes. Life was good. Life was cool.

Pray as though it is the last time you are going to be able to pray, not just in the body, but ever and ever and ever. Pray with the firm belief that you are being heard. Pray because you truly love The One you are praying to, thus, pray with true love.